ALSOP, R., AND DODKINS, G. 386

386
404
DOD.

Hertfordshire
COUNTY COUNCIL
Community Information

~9 FEB 2001

~5 MAR 2001

Forbes

22 FEB 2000

14 MAR

12 JAN 2004

18 FEB 2005

30 SEP 2000

21 OCT 2000

~9 NOV 2006

9/12

~9 JAN 2001
L32a

Please renew/return this item by the last date shown.

So that your telephone call is charged at local rate, please call the numbers as set out below:

	From Area codes 01923 or 0208:	From the rest of Herts:
Renewals:	01923 471373	01438 737373
Enquiries:	01923 471333	01438 737333
Minicom:	01923 471599	01438 737599

L32b

WORKING BOATS

WORKING
BOATS

Reliving the Romance of the Last Days of Commercial Traffic on Britain's Canals

Roger Alsop & Graham Dodkins

DAVID & CHARLES
Newton Abbot   London   North Pomfret (Vt)

Photoset and printed in Great Britain by Redwood Burn Ltd, Trowbridge, Wilts for David & Charles Publishers plc Brunel House   Newton Abbot   Devon

British Library Cataloguing in Publication Data

Dodkins, Graham
  Working boats: reliving the romance of the last days of commercial traffic on Britain's canals.
  1. Canals—Great Britain—History —20th century 2. Inland water transportation—Great Britain— Freight traffic—History—20th century
Alsop, Roger
  I. Title   II. Series
  386'.40424'0924   HE663
ISBN 0 7153 9181 X

Published in the United States of America by David & Charles Inc North Pomfret   Vermont 05053   USA

Dedicated to

P. G. I. Green, who set me on the right road. R.

Lil and Bob; a poor substitute for not giving enough back . . .
and never playing for Tottenham. G.

Contents

Illustration Credits

Colour photographs
2,3,4,5,6,7 – Harry Arnold
1 – Ted Gill
8 – Roger Alsop

Black and white photographs
5, 6, 7, 16, 17, 21, 23, 24, 25, 26, 30, 31, 33, 36, 40, 41, 43, 44, 45, 46, 50, and frontispiece – Harry Arnold
9, 11, (12 collection of), 14, 15, 19, 20, 22, 28, 48 – Graham Dodkins
3, 4, 29 – Roger Alsop
8, 13, 32, 34 – Mike Webb
18, 27, 42 – Robert Wilson
10, 35 – Michael Streat
37, 38, 47 – British Waterways
2 – Waterways World
39 – Syndication International
49 – Mike Black

Line illustrations
1 – Tony Jones
2, 3 – Roger Alsop

Foreword

by Charles Hadfield

What a book! Those who lived in working boat days will love it, but so, I think, will those who now experience the canals from a pleasure cruiser. The first will pause at every page to recall this boat, that pub, that personality, this bridge, that wharf, or the endless interest of watching lock working by professionals. The second will move, fascinated, through a strange but wonderful world.

In some ways I have seen it all. I was familiar with working boats before and during the war, and thenceforward in the pages of such records as the minute book of the Grand Union Carrying Company. I often met them at work while pleasure cruising from 1955 onwards; tried to forecast their transport future; and as a member of the British Waterways Board took part in a reluctant decision to end most of their narrow boat carrying. I knew such personalities as Tom Rolt, Kit Gayford, Sonia Smith, then a boatwoman, later Rolt's second wife, Michael Streat of Blue Line and Leslie Morton of Willow Wren. Yet I was never part of the boatman's life. It was not until 1948 that I slept on board one, to wake to the sound of an approaching Bolinder or feel the gentle wash as it passed in the mist.

Working Boats has given me many pleasures, but two are exceptional. The authors stimulate recollection, but, like me, have little time for nostalgia; and they report events accurately, but without attributing blame. I could never have written it, but I a little envy those who have. I hope it gives very many others some of the gifts that it has given me.

2   Peter Froud who gave Roger Alsop his first canal job steering hotel boats

Prelude:
Old Boats – Hotel Boats

It all started in 1957, when I was thirteen. I joined the Church Lads' Brigade in my home town of Chapel-en-le-Frith, in Derbyshire, and found my true calling, though this religious experience was not the one my mentors might have wished for. It was a revelation of quite a different kind. I discovered canals!

We boys were lucky to have, in Mr Green, a choirmaster whose interest in our spiritual welfare was not confined to teaching us 'All Things Bright and Beautiful', but manifested itself in the organisation of day trips to the Standedge Tunnel on the Huddersfield Narrow Canal, and the staircase locks at Bingley on the Leeds and Liverpool. Wide and deep, with massive gates, and alive with surging water, the locks made a big impression on me.

The contents of a small shed, discovered halfway down the flight, made a big impression on all the lads, for it housed, to our enormous glee, a double-seater privy and boys contrived to disappear, two at a time, throughout the rest of the afternoon.

The somewhat reckless Mr Green soon decided that we should see a canal from the best possible vantage point. He hired the wooden cruiser *Shirley*, from Dean's boatyard at Christleton, near Chester, one of the few companies operating a hire fleet at that time, and took us all for a canal holiday. I was apprehensive for I had never been away from home before and wondered if I would ever see our council house in Chapel and my brother and sisters again.

But we set off for Llangollen and Market Drayton along the Shropshire Union Canal and I was immediately intrigued by the peculiar, elongated craft moving purposefully by our comparatively fragile cruiser. It was the beginning of a fascination for working narrow boats that elevated boatmen, in my eyes, to the exalted position reserved among my peers for train drivers; a fascination which was to develop into an enduring passion (see Appendix I).

The beautiful Welsh Canal, with its magnificent aqueducts at Chirk and Pontycysyllte, dispelled any remaining fears I had about being away from home and on our return, Mr Green, who seemed to us boys to be very rich, added credence to our conviction by spending £250 on the purchase of *Merver*, a wooden, ex-Mersey Weaver Co narrow boat converted for pleasure use, which he intended we should use under his benevolent eye.

The boat was moored on the little used Peak Forest Canal at Whaley Bridge, just a few miles from Chapel, and it was like getting your first bike. We did it up inside, planned ambitious expeditions, plotted routes and 'borrowed' it frequently. We boated all over the North West at weekends and in the school holidays, occasionally meeting working boats on the main lines. Generally, however, the canals were deserted and what pleasure craft we saw lay neglected at their moorings. But I was hooked and never missed a trip, and I can still hear the envious cries of, 'Cor, look at them on that boat', as we slid serenly by the earth-bound gongoozlers.[1]

My already high regard for the boatmen was compounded by their friendliness, their recognition of *Merver* bringing shouts of, 'I used to work that boat', or, 'My auntie Mary, she was born in there'; and when a working boat I knew approached from the opposite direction, I would jump aboard and travel a mile or two in the company of the boat family. They told me canal stories and let me steer, not seeming to mind when I thumped the bank, and the magical Bolinder engines seemed to shake the bottoms out of the boats. They didn't tell me what to do, but I watched everything and learned a great deal about handling narrow boats. Afterwards I would run back along the towpath to catch up with my mates.

Merver was an old boat. We would lay in our bunks at night and look out through the holes in her sides. We patched her above the water-line by knocking tin plates over the holes, but we were

12

3 '. . . like getting your first bike'. Roger (left) and friends aboard
Merver

4 Plough towing heavy horse. *Saturn* towing *Jupiter* along the
Welsh Canal

baling out forty buckets of water, night and morning. Finally, a decision was taken that the underwater damage should be inspected at the British Waterways dry-dock and we set off for Northwich, on the river Weaver. Concern over the condition of the boat was tempered by excitement as we approached the famous Anderton Boat Lift and descended from the Trent and Mersey Canal to the river.

Unconcernedly rounding a bend, we were astonished to see a ship bearing down on our diminutive craft, for nobody had explained that sea-going vessels plied this major waterway. Somehow, a collision was avoided and we continued, shaken but alert, to the dock, where we received an unexpected welcome from the man in charge. 'You're not putting that on here', he said. 'If it goes on, it'll never come off.' *Merver*, the man insisted, would sag in the middle when denied the support of water. There was nothing for it; we retraced our perilous way to the Peak Forest Canal, where the old boat promptly sank in the Buxworth Arm.

Suggesting firmly that *Merver* be removed, British Waterways obligingly drained the cut and for three days, some twenty volunteers swarmed all over her, ripping off the wooden cabin and side planking and tossing the debris onto a bonfire. Then Phil Murray, a baker from nearby Chinley, came with his oxyacetylene equipment and cut off all the iron knees, leaving just the bottom on the bed of the canal. Phil later bought *Worcester*, the old tunnel tug, and we tried valiantly to get it to Buxworth, but it drew 3ft 6in with its 30hp Bolinder and we got no further than Marple.

During *Merver*'s decline, I had developed a friendship with Ken Mullins, who had built a 26ft steel boat in his back-yard at Buxworth and rolled it down the hill into the canal. Ken decided to buy a narrow boat called *Kenelm* from the Samuel Barlow Coal Co, who were still carrying at that time, and he offered me a welcome opportunity to continue boating.

On one particular trip along the Bridgewater Canal, we spotted the butty *Uranus*, painted in the same dark green Barlow colours as *Kenelm*, tied up in a remote arm at Leigh and we thought the two boats would make a handsome pair; so we continued, with the unpowered craft in tow, until we came to Plank Lane, where we were confronted by a British Waterways man, on duty at the lift bridge. To our great relief, he assumed we were a working pair and nodded us through without question. We proceeded cockily to Wigan, where we spent the night, and returned *Uranus* to her mooring the next day.

Three weeks later, I received an official looking envelope which, to my dismay, contained a solicitor's letter. It demanded, on behalf of *Uranus'* owner, one G. Waddington, '. . . the sum of five pounds, for the hire of one boat for two days'. We had been spotted playing boatmen!

The winter of 1962–3 was the hardest for many years. The canals were frozen by late December and boats were unable to move again until March, when Ken and I eagerly resumed boating. We approached the old warehouses at Preston Brook on the Bridgewater Canal one Saturday afternoon and heard the familiar, uneven throbbing of an idling Bolinder, and *Kenelm* came alongside the ex-Fellows, Morton and Clayton motor *Hawk* (See Appendix II). On board was the equally familiar Peter Froud, who regularly forged a way up to Whaley Bridge with his hotel boat *Saturn*.[2]

Peter had started his company, Canal Voyagers, shortly after the first hotel boats appeared at the 1950 Inland Waterways Association rally at Market Harborough. He bought *Saturn*, a Shropshire Union Co horse-drawn 'fly', or express boat from Alfred Matty of Tipton in December 1955 (see Appendix II). Peter had fitted a Hotchkiss cone propeller, a paddle-like contraption mounted amidships and driven by a Model B Ford paraffin engine, which enabled the boat to run almost silently, and converted to carry six paying guests, *Saturn* began operating as a hotel boat in 1958.

He was now refitting *Hawk* for the coming season, having purchased the Bolinder from the Willow Wren Canal Carrying Co. Renamed *Jupiter*, she would form a pair with *Saturn*, whose propeller and engine would eventually be removed. Half joking, I asked if he needed a steerer and to my amazement, Peter replied by asking if I could start on the following Monday. Before Ken, who would have jumped at the chance, could open his mouth, I had secured the job. Peter's wife, Marion, was to steer *Saturn* and two crew girls would prepare meals, clean the cabins, and help with the boats when necessary.

I hurried home by train, missing the 'Emil Ford and the Checkmates' concert in Runcorn, told my parents about my new job and handed in my resignation at Chapel Central railway station, where I had spent the few months since leaving school employed as a booking office clerk. Railways were my other great love and I had just passed examinations which would have taken me to the London Midland head office at Manchester Piccadilly, but there was no contest in a straight fight with canals. I kicked all that into touch when I heard that old Bolinder bobbing away, and I was back at Preston Brook on the Monday morning.

My first duty was to help Peter Froud finish the conversion of *Jupiter* in time for her inaugural cruise at the beginning of the season. As we worked, a steady stream of working boats passed the Runcorn Arm, some going empty to the British Waterways North West fleet depot a few miles down the Trent and Mersey at Anderton, and others carrying goods from Manchester to the Potteries and Wolverhampton.

Work was interrupted one morning when Peter introduced me to a very large man who had called at the yard. 'This is Gordon Waddington, he's got a fleet of short boats and barges', he said. As we shook hands, my thoughts flashed back to the escapade with *Uranus* and my face burned with the shame of it, but Mr Waddington made no mention of the affair. Had he failed to connect me with the incident, or was he just being discreet? Too embarrassed to own up, I made an excuse and left the two men talking about narrow boats.

When the day of the inaugural cruise arrived, the boats were filled with well-wishing friends and local dignitaries and *Jupiter*, towing *Saturn* behind, moved off majestically along the cut. The celebrations were in full swing when the Bolinder seized and a very embarrassed Peter Froud trekked back to Preston Brook to fetch a spare boat to tow the illustrious pair back to base.

From their departure point at Chester, the boats were scheduled to travel to Llangollen, Whaley Bridge and Stourport; but when the first paying guests of the season arrived to begin their cruise on the Welsh Canal, *Jupiter*'s engine was still inoperative and my career as captain of hotel boats started inauspiciously as the spare boat was again employed as a tug. The Bolinder was finally repaired en route, but *Jupiter*'s 3ft 3in draught was to prove an equally serious handicap.

Saturn, a barrel-shaped 'Shroppie', slipped easily along the shallow cut, but *Jupiter* bumped and scraped the bottom of the canal. Everyone gave a hand bow-hauling, but progress was laboured and halted, eventually, at Frankton, where *Jupiter*'s compliment of six passengers, with as much as they could carry, clambered onto *Saturn*'s roof. The Hotchkiss cone propelled the party on towards Llangollen and *Jupiter* was left behind. At the end of an exhausting day, Peter received a distress call and drove out in his van to ferry six weary guests back to their beds aboard the disabled motor, an operation which was repeated several times before we reached Frankton again on the return journey.

On a subsequent trip, we experimented and discovered that *Saturn* was capable of towing *Jupiter* along the shallow sections if the latter's load was eased as before and her ballast shifted forward to lift the stern end out of the water. To those gongoozlers who could distinguish one type of narrow boat from another, the site of a butty towing a motor must have looked as incongruous as a plough towing a heavy horse. But it was a mixed blessing because at Llangollen, it took a day and a half to turn *Jupiter* around in the silted-up winding hole.

With the early mishaps behind us, the season settled into an uneventful routine. The passengers' day began at eight with a cup of tea in bed, followed by breakfast in the saloon. The boats set off after the meal and coffee was served mid-morning, while the boats were under way. After a break for lunch, we carried on again until evening and had dinner at about half past seven. We kept to our itinerary without haste and I enjoyed the leisurely pace. Everything else seemed to be going faster and faster, but we had time to turn around and have another look. And it was always sunny.

But my recollection of the period, an unbroken succession of long, hot summer days is, no doubt, time's old illusion; a heat haze shimmers over the field of my memory, obscuring the flaws in the landscape.

My second season on the hotel boats was destined to be more eventful and began with a new arrival. Peter appeared on the towpath at Stewpony on the Staffs and Worcester Canal with Patricia Hayes, a seventeen year old who had answered his advertisement in *The Lady* for a replacement crew girl. By July, when we headed for the Inland Waterways Association rally at Stratford upon Avon, Pat and I were close friends.

The 1964 rally was to be a celebration of the Stratford Canal's restoration and an official reopening ceremony was to be performed by the Queen Mother. The occasion had been incorporated into the hotel boats' itinerary, with *Jupiter* and *Saturn* running from Long Buckby on the Grand Union, to the Avon, but when we turned into the canal at Kingswood Junction, we were halted by an armada of diverse craft, each waiting their turn to work down the narrow Lapworth flight. The chaos continued below the locks, where we picked our way through an obstacle course of boats, aground, broken down and abandoned. The National Trust's resources of men and water were stretched to the limit when Peter turned up, riding a tractor, to mount a one-man rescue operation, towing breakdowns and pulling boats out of the mud.

Progress was slow, but we found ourselves in good company. *Coleshill* and *Cygnus*, a pair of narrow boats operated by the Willow Wren company, were taking the opportunity presented by the rally to advertise the fact that our canals were still being used for their original purpose of carrying goods. Steerers Ray and Margaret White were delivering sugar and a consignment of Japanese motor cycles to Stratford.[3] It took two and a half days to negotiate the thirteen miles and we experienced a wonderful sensation of freedom when, finally, we sailed onto the deep and wide waters of the Avon. *Coleshill* and *Cygnus* were the first commercial narrow boats to arrive in the town for thirty-five years and they were greeted with champagne and wild applause.

On a warm evening a few days after the rally, Pat and I were again tying up the boats above Buckby top lock in readiness for a changeover of passengers, when we were greeted by Jack Hatchard, an old acquaintance, who had stopped his working boat *Comet* for the night on his way back empty to the Willow Wren depot at Braunston.

We decided to adjourn to the New Inn and crossed the canal by the Watling Street road bridge at the tail of the lock. The door facing the cut opened into a tiny, dark enclave and after buying our drinks in an adjoining room, we settled down on a wooden bench by the juke-box. Accompanied by *The Bachelors'* 'Ramona', a great favourite with the several boaters who had chosen to stop over at Long Buckby, Jack told us about his job. He worked his single motor alone, carrying coal from the Midland collieries to the Hertfordshire paper mills; then he reloaded at Brentford and returned north with timber, wheat, or metal. It was hard going on his own and he was fed up with it.

I, in turn, told Jack all about the idle pleasures of hotel boating, adding that I needed a change as well, and after more drinks and further lamentations, it became quite clear to me that the only solution was for us to swap jobs. Jack offered little resistance to the idea, and when Pat agreed to go with me, the ensuing celebrations lasted until closing time.

The harsh light of the following morning brought with it the realisation that arrangements had still to be made. Dennis Clarke, Willow Wren manager at Braunston, and Peter Froud, were contacted by telephone and as each of the parties was known by the others, the transfer was quickly completed. Pat and I were to take *Comet* on to Willow Wren's yard at Braunston, while Jack took immediate charge of the hotel boats.

He stripped *Comet*'s cabin, taking all his domestic utensils and his bedding, including the mattress! The only thing he left behind was the new Calor Gas stove which he, like many of the boat people, by that time used for cooking. They were cleaner and more practical for this purpose than the old solid fuel ranges which traditionally stood on the left hand side as you stepped down into the cabin. Pat, especially, was pleased to have inherited such a luxury, but the bottle gas stoves were not blessed with the same versatility as the old ranges. The constantly burning traditional version kept the cabins beautifully warm and the steerer, at the mercy of the elements above the waist, could stand on the cabin step, close the doors behind him, draw the hatch up to his hip, and give thanks for the glow caressing his feet and legs.

We gathered up our own meagre belongings and wished Jack good luck then I started *Comet*'s engine, stepped onto the counter, and headed up the cut to a strange new world.

5   Ian Kemp (left), responsible for restoring *Comet*, looks on while Roger Alsop trims the cargo

6 *Comet* loaded for the last time at Gopsall Wharf – with coal for Croxley Mill

1

Comet

In July 1985, I went back to the cut to relive an adventure; to rediscover that 'strange new world', and recall my days as a boatman in the mid-sixties, when trade was enjoying its last, desperate fling on the canals of England. And I went back to see how the cut had changed since its takeover by the leisure industry.

In the sixties, the commonest cargo was coal. We loaded at three Midland collieries and took it some 100 miles down the Oxford and Grand Union Canals to cut side destinations in Hertfordshire. What better way then, to jog the memory, than to take a pair of narrow boats, the same pair that I captained in the sixties, load them with coal in the Midlands as Willow Wren had done, and follow the old trading route south. And how better to see how the cut had changed since its exploitation in the holiday brochures and the travel guides.

I wanted to find out if the docks and wharves, the depots and the boatyards that were busy with commerce in 1964, were decaying and obsolete in the eighties. What had happened to the boat people? Were they still to be found in the pubs and at the old stopping places? Or had their migration to homes and work 'on the land' wasted away their once self contained world, leaving the cut to the holiday makers and the enthusiasts?

Was it still possible to make the journey with a fully loaded pair? Would the canals be too shallow now that a channel was no longer scoured by the regular passage of the deep draughted working boats? Would a pair of 70ft narrow boats be able to thread their way along canals over populated by fleets of hire craft? Were the locks in a reasonable state of repair?

In the sixties, we worked up to seventeen hours a day in order to complete the trips in the three or four days demanded by the company. How would we compare now for stamina and efficiency? On the threshold of my journey, these were the questions and uncertainties that crowded into my mind, but many questions had been answered and many problems solved before I even got to the starting line.

It had seemed a good and simple idea to retrace my steps and re-enact, using the same boats and carrying a similar cargo, one of the trips I had undertaken for Willow Wren. But I have to admit that after a little thought, prompted by the scepticism of those around me, there did seem to be a few obstacles! I wasn't certain if the boats I had captained had survived the intervening years; if they had, where would I find them and would their owners allow me to use them for what might seem a scatterbrain expedition? How should I go about obtaining forty odd tons of coal and, if I took it south as Willow Wren had done, who would want it when it got there? Undeterred, I decided to take one step at a time and hope that I could resolve each problem in turn.

My first task was to track down the boats! I had worked with three during my stay with Willow Wren; the small Woolwich motor boat *Comet*, which I kept throughout, was paired first with the station butty *Dabchick* and, later, the large Woolwich *Barnes* (see Appendix II). *Comet*, I felt, was the linchpin to the whole operation. Being able to use the motor I had steered throughout my stint as a working boatman was not essential for the execution of my scheme, any sound narrow boat in working trim would do, but *Comet* was the evocation of those exciting days and to undertake the trip without her seemed pointless.

I had left the boat in basically hale condition when I quit Willow Wren in February 1965, although she was showing signs of wear and tear. She still wore the drab blue of British Waterways, almost two years after Willow Wren's takeover of the nationalised fleet, an indication that the company had kept the boat fully employed without docking, managing only to paint out the old BW lettering on the cabin sides.

Early in 1967 I had bought the large Woolwich motor *Chiswick* from Willow Wren and while working on her engine at Braunston

I was saddened to see *Comet* languishing in the reservoir and looking in a very sorry state indeed. Much later, in the summer of 1979, at Norton Canes on the Birmingham Canal Navigations, I saw a small Woolwich motor, bearing no name, which had undergone extensive and expert restoration. I recognised the boat's owner, a tall young man with lank brown hair and a chunky polo-neck, as Ian Kemp, who had approached me some years before with an offer for *Chiswick*. My delight, on learning that the boat rescued by Ian's commitment and expertise was none other than *Comet*, was coupled with relief, for I had thought it doubtful that she had survived the reservoir at Braunston.

Five years after that fortuitous reunion, I was desperate to find *Comet* again, for the boat was central to my plan. I telephoned Canal Transport Services at Norton Canes, asking if they knew Ian's whereabouts and was told that he was restoring the Josher *Shad* for the Boat Museum at Ellesmere Port. I rang the museum immediately and explained my scheme to a rather bemused Ian who, despite my earlier refusal to part with *Chiswick*, was gracious enough to show some interest and we arranged a meeting.

On a bright, cold Sunday morning in January, over a cup of tea in the Boat Museum restaurant, I sketched out my plan. In his quiet, earnest way, Ian asked some pertinent questions and expressed his concern should the trip turn out to be some kind of media event. I did my best to reassure him that one of the aims of the exercise was to try to cover the distance in the time allowed to the Willow Wren boaters in the sixties and that drumming up media interest, with its pursuant delays, interruptions and distractions, would not serve such a purpose well. He seemed satisfied with my motives, giving his tentative agreement to make *Comet* available, and I had taken the first, and most important, step in getting the expedition off the ground.

Tucked away at the business end of the Museum, her bow nosing up to the dry dock where much of the hard graft of boat restoration is carried out, *Comet* was in immaculate condition, looking good enough to command a position on the other side of the Pump House alongside the floating exhibits. She had seldom enjoyed such care and attention during her chequered life. From the euphoria of the mid-thirties, through numerous grand, but ill-fated revivals, to the irrevocable decline of carrying at the end of the sixties, the old boat had seen it all.

Comet and her original butty *Meteor*, were one of twenty-four iron composite pairs built by Harland & Wolff in 1935 as part of the Grand Union Canal Carrying Co's massive expansion programme. The company built up a fleet of 373 craft, but it proved difficult to find enough crews and many of the boats remained idle. In terms of traffic gained, the expansion was successful, but money had been borrowed to finance the new boats and the company was never able to achieve a profit. Some surplus craft were disposed of, but *Comet* was still in the fleet when the company was nationalised on 1st January 1948.

Later, Fellows, Morton & Clayton, the largest remaining private carrying company, went into voluntary liquidation and their fleet of 172 boats joined the 250 former GUCCC craft to form the British Waterways South Eastern Division carrying fleet. But the canals were suffering from lack of maintenance, traffic had declined to its lowest ever level, and it was still difficult to find crews. The fleet was now too big so some craft were downgraded to maintenance boats, some were sold to private carriers, notably Willow Wren, and many more were sunk in Harefield Flash, a former gravel pit adjoining the Grand Union. Boats were abandoned in small groups all over the canal system and, by 1962, the fleet was reduced to forty five pairs.

Somehow, *Comet* survived the holocaust, and when the nationalised fleet was finally disbanded in 1963, she was one of about forty craft leased by Willow Wren. A brief renaissance followed and when I ran *Comet*, from July 1964 until February the next year, the company were running about forty five pairs; but they soon faced a major problem.

Willow Wren's most important traffic was coal from Pooley Hall colliery, on the Coventry Canal, to John Dickinson's paper mill at Croxley Green, on the Grand Union, and when I saw *Comet* abandoned in the reservoir at Braunston in January 1967, the company had just delivered its last load under the contract. It never recovered from this setback and early in 1968, *Comet* was among three dozen pairs repossessed by British Waterways for non-payment of the hire charges. In March the boats were moved to the Wendover Arm of the Grand Union and offered for sale by tender, with preference given to genuine carriers. With a couple of exceptions, all the boats were in deplorable condition, their fittings stripped by souvenir hunters and the motors without engines, but *Comet*, and the butty *Betelgeuse*, were rescued by Tony and Trevor Jones who were setting up Stroudwater Carriers.

Comet, like the rest, had no engine, and no mast and stands; but the cabin was reasonable and the boat retained propeller, swan's neck, side sheets and cratch board, with only six or eight bottom planks in need of replacement. One fine summer day, while Trevor's girlfriend, '. . . dressed up for an afternoon on a 3 metre yacht', sunned herself on the cabin top, the brothers set off bow-hauling and punting the pair along the Wendover Arm, and at Bulbourne, boatman Roger Hatchard arrived with his immaculate 'Josher' to provide the first of the tows required to reach Charity Dock, Bedworth, where they were to undergo a major refit.

Trevor: Joe Gilbert was a wonderful character and we hit it off immediately. He could do anything – from refitting narrow boats, to respraying Mini Coopers, to rebuilding diesel lorry engines. He had a forge, he had a machine shop, he had a dry dock with a selection of marvellous and ancient jacks, and he had a yard full of unbelievable junk. He could do practically anything mechanical, and Jesse Owen turned the boats out beautifully.

Tony: We were fortunate that at Charity Dock the painting of the boats was considered an integral part of docking. Generally, Jesse Owen would tell *us* what the painting should be and his work far exceeded our modest specifications. That the periods of docking invariably exceeded the stipulated time and led to occasional acrimony, is a feature of boat or shipyard life whether Charity Dock or Swan Hunter.

Tony and Trevor took Joe and Jesse over to Braunston, where they poked around in the old Willow Wren store and came out with a set of mast and stands; then they bought an engine from Lister's at Dursley.

Trevor: Then came the great day when we were ready to start the engine for the first time – it was a circus. There were a lot of boatmen around the yard for one reason or another, and we had them all working on that Lister for a whole afternoon, just to get it to swing over. It was factory reconditioned – and it was tight! We got to the stage where we had two on the handle, and one on the roof with a rope on the handle, all trying to co-ordinate and pull at the same time and, eventually, that wonderful moment came when the engine fired off and set up into that sound that was to be the rhythm of my life for the next year or so.

So the boat was given a new lease of life – and put back to work. The Birmingham & Midland Canal Carrying Co had resumed the Croxley coal run and, in January 1969, *Comet* and *Betelgeuse* were employed on a sub-contract basis. Trevor's previous boating experience was limited to pleasure cruising, and a trip from Coventry to Braunston with Willow Wren boatman Ted Ward.

Trevor: He was called 'Mad Ted', and he had a reputation as an engine smasher, which I could understand, having seen him operate. He was rough on his boats. He was around Joe's yard and Joe Gilbert says, 'You ought to go along with him and learn some stuff. It might not be good – but go ahead'. So my friend John Rogers and I went with 'Mad Ted' and we learned the 'road' as far as Braunston and handled his boats empty.

With this meagre experience, Trevor and John loaded 50 tons, at the princely rate of 15/4d (77p) per ton, at Gopsall Wharf on the Ashby Canal.

Trevor: Gopsall Wharf was nothing more than a triangular field. It had a piled wall, dredged out, and a diesel powered conveyor belt. The lorry would tip into the hopper, the conveyor would bring the coal up – and you would stand on the gunnel and control the position of your boat with your legs, while hanging onto the end of the conveyor. If there was a pretty good wind, it was hard to control things and you would find the conveyor tipping coal down the back of your neck, down the tops of your Wellington boots, into the cut and just about anywhere else.

Wanting to appear good, experienced boatmen they unnecessarily sheeted up. Trevor got *Comet* underway and John attached the snubber to the fore-end of the butty and made his way back along the top planks. As the motor took up the slack, the butty heeled and started to move. John lost his balance and plunged into the cut, losing his glasses in the process. It was the first of a series of disasters.

Trevor: It was the middle of the afternoon, near Fenny Stratford, and we'd had nothing to eat. No experienced boatman would stop for a meal, but we did. I pulled over to the bank and stepped off with a long line and took a turn around a small tree to bring the boats to a standstill. I'd shut down the motor, but I hadn't thrown it out of gear, and *Comet* kept going and going. The tree wasn't holding and the rope, which was tangled around on the ground, was running through my hands. I let go – and stopped a loaded pair of narrow boats with a line that had three turns around my ankle. Nothing was broken, but the skin was crushed to the bone.

John had been a big handicap without his glasses, and as I needed to rest up, he decided to hitch-hike home to Stroud to get a spare pair. I spent the night in near delirium on the boats. Next morning, I shouted for help, and some people on a nearby bridge came down and got me to a doctor who dressed the ankle and sent me back to the boats. John returned next day with his spare glasses and we made it somehow to Croxley.

I asked at the Mill for some more dressings, but they took one look at the ankle and despatched me, in the company van, to Watford Hospital, where I was taken care of by a Pakistani doctor who spoke very little English, and had a very peculiar idea of medicine. He decided, though the ankle wasn't broken, to put a plaster cast on it, saying something about how, during the Spanish Civil War, they had used plaster for treating wounds in the field! Seeing me covered in coal dust, I suppose he thought that I wasn't going to keep things clean. That afternoon I was back at Croxley unloading and the cast was already broken in several places.

We dragged ourselves back to Braunston and called Anthony, who was ready to climb the walls. He'd picked up a rumour that I'd been seen with my leg in plaster and he'd called all the depots and people he could think of in an effort to contact us. He came down to Braunston and he was furious; we were filthy, the boats were filthy, and we had taken two and a half weeks trying to get one load delivered. He gave our arses a good kicking.

When Birmingham & Midland lost the Croxley contract, the boats lay idle for a couple of months until the Ashby Canal Association managed to negotiate the resumption of deliveries to John Dickinson's with the result that Stroudwater Carriers' boats, along with some of Willow Wren's remaining craft were, against all the odds, employed carrying once more down the Grand Union. The company struggled to secure additional work, but endless leads resulted in endless dead ends and when it proved impossible to get reliable mates, *Betelgeuse* was laid up and *Comet* ran as a single motor. Soon Dickinson's announced their intention to change part of their steam raising plant to fuel oil, with the little coal still required coming by lorry, and *Comet* began her last run from Gopsall to Croxley, with 22 tons 10 cwt, on 20th August 1970, just six days before the Willow Wren pair *Redshank* and *Ara* carried the final load.

It had already been decided to wind up the carrying activities of the Willow Wren fleet, which had dwindled to six pairs, and about a month later the three immaculate Blue Line pairs carried their last loads to the Jam 'Ole. *Comet* had been one of the handful of boats still trading at the end of 200 years of narrow boat carrying on the canals.

However, that wasn't quite the end of her working life. During 1971 she was employed on towage and the movement of plant for pipe-laying along the Coventry Canal and in December was contracted to tow two boats down to Gloucester in connection with bridge work there. On this trip, at the suggestion of Nick Hill of the Ashby Canal Association, *Comet* was loaded with 14 tons of coal at Clifton Wharf, Rugby and after the boats were delivered, the whole load was sold retail along the Sharpness Canal.

Tony Jones: That the trade was so successful is due to the nature of the locals who are still very conscious of the canal. The progress of the 'coal boat' would be broadcast via the cut telegraph, the lock and bridge men being at one with the rural community. That first load I sold mostly at Fretherne Wharf, Frampton, weighing and bagging half-hundred-weights which went off on farm wagons and cycle cross-bars. On the odd deal I got a gallon jar of cider 'to keep the dust down', and from the Cadburys factory, a bag of crumb 'for the kids'.

The night before Christmas Eve I cycled home leaving *Comet*, clean swept, in the charge of the bridgeman, with my takings stuffed down my socks.

Comet and *Betelgeuse*, crewed by Jim and Dinah Marshall who had joined Tony from Birmingham & Midland, continued to pioneer the retail coal trade, loading at Gopsall, Anglesey Basin (probably the last boats to load there) and Pelsall, on the BCN. But with the rising cost of coal reducing profit margins, Jim and Dinah ran *Betelgeuse* as a horse-drawn trip boat in Chester and *Comet* spent her summers as a camping boat, with hordes of noisy children clambering all over her dignity.

Ian Kemp was engaged and when the winter coal trade resumed the boats worked over a wide area in the hope that others would follow the lead, but it was often difficult to make reasonable headway until reaching the more reliable Worcester and Birmingham Canal. The bottoms were being knocked out of the boats and it was impossible to guarantee delivery dates to customers. Trade suffered, and after struggling on for a couple of years, Ian decided to lease a pair from Birmingham & Midland, believing that loading at Stourport, Worcester, or Birmingham would improve things. Tony soldiered on before finally giving up in favour of tripping. *Comet* carried her last load of coal, 19 tons 3 cwt of Bagworth nuts, on 8th October 1976, and was subsequently sold to Ian Kemp.

> **Tony Jones**: In *Comet* we had a really lovely boat; she swam beautifully. In my opinion, the small Woolwich class were an excellent all round boat for carrying capacity, handling and maintenance (until Dutch elm disease sent the price of elm up). The trads can laud their precious Joshers all they like and, whatever their much vaunted capacity, I found the handling of a light Admiral rather inferior to a garden shed.[1] Given a good road, the big Woolwich's high sides would be an advantage for loading, but they didn't handle well. With her 22b hp Lister HA2 and 3:1 reduction, once *Comet* tucked the counter down she'd pull like a trojan.

The boat was looking in poor condition once more, but eighteen months passed before Ian found time to begin any restoration work. He took her to Norton Canes, where he got her onto the bank and into the rolling shed at a reasonable rate, intending to reclad the cabin and patch up a dent in the counter; but one thing led to another and in the end a simple five week job took two and a half years to complete. The final touch was the blue and yellow livery of British Waterways (see Appendix III).

> **Ian Kemp**: I chose this 'non-traditional' colour scheme be-

32

cause I consider the GUCCC boats to have been in their best condition during this period and because it was unfashionable. Every other boat on the cut seemed to be painted red, yellow and green.

So, after almost fifty years of swaying fortunes, *Comet* was restored to her prime.

7 *Comet* undergoing restoration at Norton Canes
8 *Barnes* at Braunston in her Willow Wren days – Mrs Ted Barratt steering

2

Barnes – And a Cargo

I knew that my first butty, *Dabchick*, was a non-starter. In 1964, Joyce and Peter Fox were running Peter Froud's newly acquired hotel boats *Mabel* and *Forget-me-Not* and they subsequently started up on their own. They bought *Dabchick*, and the motor *Mallard* from Willow Wren in 1966 and had the pair converted into hotel boats at Blue Line's yard at Braunston. Joyce and Peter were still in business and one could hardly fill a hotel boat with coal! Besides, it wouldn't look right.[1]

That left *Barnes*. My first tentative enquiries were answered with the discouraging rumour that there had been a fire and the butty had been destroyed! A couple of days later I was absently scanning the 'Boats for sale' columns in my waterways magazine, distracted by the thought that my scheme might not even get off the ground, when I found myself reading an advertisement offering *Barnes* for sale. I rang the number and learned that the boat had, in fact, survived an attack by vandals on her partner *Badsey*. The pair had been lying on the Slough Arm of the Grand Union when the motor's pigeon box had been ripped off and a lighted torch dropped into the engine hole. The old carpets protecting the engine from the winter weather had burned, melting the electrics. The alternator, batteries and oil pump had been destroyed but, thankfully, the fuel did not ignite and the boats escaped with £1,500 worth of damage. Beginning to feel that my scheme might be destined to succeed after all, I outlined my proposals to *Barnes'* owner and arranged to meet him at his supermarket in Godalming.

It had been a busy Good Friday morning in the shop and David Vickers was leaning wearily against the glass entrance doors reading a paper when I pulled up outside. I followed his Volvo estate to a secluded mooring by Broadford Bridge on the river Wey and there, in the pale Easter sunshine, unconverted, with her big, bluff bow standing up out of the water, was *Barnes*.

We sat in the butty's cabin, my home through the winter of 1964–5, and I explained my mission, with David unable to control the irresistible urge to jump up and peer out of the hatch at the sound of every approaching boat.

Barnes, like *Comet*, had been purchased from British Waterways and rehabilitated. Clive Stevens had stripped off the back cabin and rebuilt it, with a 4ft 6in extension housing a cooker and sink unit, and set the butty to work with the motor *Battersea* on the coal run from Gopsall to Croxley. She was sold again in 1973 to Jill and David Humphries, who reunited her with her original motor *Badsey* and David Vickers bought the pair in 1979. He related with relish his family's exploits with the big boats and declared an interest, providing satisfactory arrangements could be made, in seeing *Barnes* loaded with coal once more.

The boats then, in principle at least, were secured and now I had to find a cargo. I had been reading about a chap named Andy Rothen, who had built up a successful coal business at Atherstone Wharf on the Coventry Canal. The stories concerned his fight to retain the wharf despite the efforts of the local area BWB to repossess it. When I spoke to Andy he was hopeful that he would be able to continue in busines and he quoted some prices. Buying the coal wholesale in this way would entail an outlay of around £3,000 and though a decent profit from the retail sale could be expected, it was a considerable sum. Customers would have to be found for the forty odd tons we planned to carry and that would mean a great deal of hard and time consuming work, hawking for outlets. All in all, a risky business.

Some time before the idea of the trip had been formulated, I had met Sue and John Yates who regularly sold house coal along the Grand Union from their narrow boats *Barnham* and *Angel*. I telephoned them at Battlebridge Basin in London and arranged to call, so on a clear, mild November night, I crossed a muddy car park somewhere behind King's Cross station and knocked on a corrugated iron door. It was opened by a tall, shadowy figure who, to my great relief, turned out to be John Yates, and I was led along a narrow stone sill at the base of a high brick wall. The sill formed a cat-walk between the wall and the dark waters of the basin and in the watery moonlight I could see an unbroken line of real narrow boats, both converted and in working trim, their stern ends tethered to iron rings set into the cat-walk and their bows stretching out towards the centre of the wide basin.

Set into the wall was a recess housing a number of old bicycles and a door leading into a communal wash-room; a washing machine and tumble drier stood inside and, in an inner room, a bath. There was a blackboard on the wall where residents reserved their bath-times in chalk. Every available space aboard Sue and John's converted narrow boat *Antares* was utilised. A solid writing desk sat squarely, its top covered with papers and tools; their small son's train set wound around the floor and shelves overflowed with books. Stepping gingerly among the rails, I sank into an ample leather armchair, while John folded himself into a canvas collapsible and Sue prepared their evening meal in the ·adjoining galley.

The Yates, I learned, operate as agents for Ashby Canal Transport Ltd, a company that evolved from the trading section of the Ashby Canal Association. It was this body that renegotiated the contract to supply coal to Dickinson's mill at Croxley in 1969, when the Willow Wren and Stroudwater Carriers boats were sub-contractors. After Dickinson's ended the traffic in 1970, the trading section of the Association became an Authorised Coal Dealer, under the name of Ashby Canal Transport Ltd, and began using factors to operate a retail service to canal side customers around the southern waterways.

Sue and John took over the Grand Union run formerly operated by Tam and Di Murrell, and the Thames run operated by Nick Hill's *Jaguar*. One Thames trip, loading at Brentford and selling up to Lechlade, is undertaken each summer; then runs commence at eight week intervals through the winter on the southern Grand Union, with the boats loading at Hawkesbury Junction. The coal is weighed and bagged en route and sales start south of Leighton

Buzzard, with the boats getting ever lighter as they progress towards their final delivery at Hackney.

John Yates: It is regular and it pays relatively well; and it is dreadfully hard work. But the boats, to us, are acceptable juggernauts, disrupting the environment less than heavy lorries and fuel costs on the canal are one fifth those of road haulage.

But Sue and John face a dilemma that has dogged generations of boat families.

John: We are unable to expand further without running into a problem – Joshua's education. He is now five and has always lived on the boats. His school in Islington has been very co-operative and has not, so far, objected to him missing the odd week or two in the belief that he is learning as much from his varied life as he would in the classroom. However, if we increased the frequency of the runs, I feel that his schooling would suffer and it really would not be fair to sacrifice him in this way. We could put a crew on the boats and join them from time to time, but we enjoy it all so much and would hate sitting at home taking phone messages. But perhaps water transport demands it of us . . .

It was agreed that the Thames run might be rearranged to suit the purposes of my scheme. If the lorries delivered the coal to Hawkesbury, instead of Brentford, *Comet* and *Barnes* could carry it south to London where it could be transhipped into John's pair for delivery up river. The route, down the northern Oxford and the Grand Union, was the one taken in the sixties, with the loading point at Hawkesbury just a mile south of Newdigate colliery, where I loaded on my first Willow Wren trip. The Newdigate coal was taken to the Colne Valley Sewage Works at Rickmansworth and it would be a simple matter, as we passed the place, to compare our time with that taken in the sixties. After unloading at Rickmansworth we had continued to Brentford to collect a back-

9 Sue and John Yates with Josh

load, so we would be covering exactly the same ground in 1985.

I had got the boats and the cargo, now it was a matter of ironing out the details. I inspected *Barnes'* hull, groping around in the hold among bicycles and camp beds, lifting the snow-heavy cloths to allow a shaft of light to penetrate the gloom. She seemed sound enough. Plans for towing the butty up to Hawkesbury were laid, scrapped, and laid again, and an itinerary for the trip was worked out. We arranged to load on 24th July, the 21st anniversary of my first trip. As we only intended to make a single trip British Waterways obligingly waived the necessity for commercial licences and pleasure licences were obtained. Insurance was arranged, but not before a full and minutely detailed explanation of our activities had been demanded in writing by *Barnes'* insurers and the haggling over participants' expenses was amicably settled.

Then, at the eleventh hour, John rang to say that we could not load on the proposed day because the pits would be on their annual holiday. At this stage I thought it was all up, but after some desperate 'phone calls, the whole trip was rearranged, with the final itinerary looking like this:

Badsey and *Barnes* depart Broadford Bridge	7.7.85
Travel via Wey, Thames and Grand Union to Bridgewater Boats, Berkhamsted. Arrive	9.7
Roger departs with boats for Long Buckby (thence on to Hawkesbury)	15.7
Meet Ian and Marion Kemp with *Comet* and Harry Arnold at Hawkesbury	18.7
Comet and *Barnes* load	19.7
Arrive Brentford (hopefully)	24.7

3

Buckby Wharf

At last I found myself at Buckby Wharf, sitting in the very corner of the New Inn where my original adventure had begun twenty one years before. On the following day, we would rendezvous with *Comet* and take aboard our cargo, but now I had a moment to draw breath, to assimilate my surroundings and begin to take stock of the modern cut.

The pub had been gutted! The succession of little adjoining rooms had made way for a long bar which stood at the centre of an open plan interior amid a plethora of counterfeit beams and stud-work. There were brown carpet tiles covering the flag stones and chintzy curtains at the windows. The old plaster walls, whose imperfections were largely camouflaged with heavy artex, were adorned with paintings of greyhounds in gilt frames and little wooden wall lights with red tassled shades.

Outside, where the A5 road bridge carries articulated lorries thundering across the canal, the only apparent alteration to the exterior of the old pub was a low, ugly extension, complete with bottle-glass windows, running the length of the once flat and unfussy façade.

Next door to the New Inn, the good looking two storey house of red brick still stood with a little shop at its side. The pair were built in 1922 by James Lovelock, then landlord of the pub, and the shop sold groceries and household goods and all manner of equipment for the working boats – coils of cotton and hemp line, tackle and feed for the boat horses, paraffin lamps and paraffin. But the shop's most famous commodity, as Tom Rolt described in *Narrow Boat*, was a can for carrying water:

41

This insignificant little shop standing beside Buckby top lock has customers all over England; there is scarcely a boat trading down to Brentford or Paddington Basin that does not carry a Buckby can, and I have recognised their distinctive style on boat-decks in every county in the Midlands. For many of the boatmen they are the only outlet for their instinctive love of colour, because the large carrying companies who handle the bulk of London–Birmingham traffic no longer budget for castles and flowers, but paint their boats in uniform colours of blue and maroon or red and green. The cans are expensive, but it would never occur to the boatman that a galvanised bucket would answer the purpose equally well, because he has a different and truer sense of values. So he buys his painted can by instalments, paying a shilling or two each time he passes by, the agreement being one of mutual trust.

The old shopkeeper shuffled out of the back regions in response to the clang of the doorbell. It was obvious that he had been a broad, powerfully built man before age had bent him, also, from the way that he peered at us, that he was almost blind. At first he was inclined to be surly, but when we explained that we wished to purchase a water-can and dipper, and had duly admired them, he unbent towards us, seating himself on a stool behind the counter. He used to paint the cans himself, he told us, but he confessed sadly that his sight no longer enabled him to do such fine work, and now they were painted for him at Braunston . . . All the while he was talking he fiddled with a small brush, brushing his ears and his bushy moustache, a curious mannerism which attracted us with an awful, hypnotic fascination. When eventually we took our leave of him he showed us the door, still talking volubly and by this time brushing his shaggy eyebrows.[1]

At one time, the cans were painted by Lovelock's niece Matilda and it is alleged that the old man kept her a virtual prisoner, not allowing her any respite from the painting. A recent visitor to the shop, a man now in his seventies, says that he and Matilda had been in love and wanted to marry, but old Lovelock would have none of it and sent him packing. Poor Matilda hanged herself along the canal.

In 1950, ten years after Rolt wrote his evocative description, Lovelock was taken seriously ill and another niece, Ethel Griffiths, and her husband Tom, moved from London to nurse the old man and look after the shop. Mrs Griffiths was born beside the canal at Yelverton, on the Leicester section of the Grand Union, where her parents kept the Boat Inn. She left home to work the horse-drawn narrow boats carrying grain from London to Birmingham and Leicester. Tom was a wide barge man from London. When Lovelock died, he left the shop to Ethel. She and Tom concentrated on selling groceries and the cans disappeared, but the boaters didn't desert the place. In the sixties the boat women shopped for a whole family, *and* passed on the latest news, in the time it took their boats to work through the lock outside.

Tom Griffiths died at Christmas in 1977 and Ethel decided, at the age of eighty two, after running the shop for twenty seven years, to retire. She was asked if she would miss the canal world, and after gazing for a long moment at the lock outside the window she replied, 'It's been my whole life'.[2]

The property was sold to purchasers who proclaimed no interest at all in the cut, but was sold again within two years to Shirley and Maurice Ginger who were 'nutty about canals'. They started boating in 1970, bought an old wooden butty and then had a boat built at Braunston. Shirley, an artist, took up traditional canal painting and the hunt began for a canal-side property from which she could sell her wares. A long and frustrating search finally ended at Long Buckby, which they regarded as 'just perfect'. The Gingers moved in a week before Easter 1981, but it wasn't until they found a box full of old deeds and letters that it really dawned on them that they had bought the original Buckby can shop.

Familiar, now, with the shop's history, and aware that there were few places along the cut where boaters could buy provisions, Shirley and Maurice decided to carry on selling groceries along

10 Ethel Griffiths serving in the shop at Buckby

11 Shirley Ginger – she carries on the Buckby shop tradition

with the canal ware; but it was difficult to justify staying open during the long winter months, when only a handful of hardy pleasure boaters braved the elements. Nobody came from the fifty or so houses at Long Buckby unless they had forgotten something at the supermarket and the trickle of customers who stopped their cars to buy sweets or cigarettes were too few. In the summertime, however, the little shop is busy and colourful. A rush nowadays is not precipitated by the arrival of a big spending working boat family, but a pair of camping boats with a couple of dozen kids in orange life jackets, anxious to spend their pocket money. They are drawn, no doubt, by the ice cream advertisements swinging and fluttering in the breeze, and by the name of the shop, for 'Gingers' Stores' sounds as though it must be full of treats.

The old mullioned shop window, so rotten that it was demolished with a pair of pliers, had been replaced by a far less attractive, but more practical, plate glass, double glazed job with aluminium window frames, which displayed Shirley's canal ware and drawings to their best advantage. Little had been done to destroy the old fashioned interior. The original wooden counters and shelves were painted cream and a partition still screened the tiny space that Lovelock used as his office. Shirley had turned it into her studio, her upturned brushes standing in a jam jar among pots of paint and her Buckby cans hanging from ceiling hooks originally put up for the same purpose by the old man. All the usual grocery lines, from cans of peaches to toilet rolls, were stocked, along with real ale, fudge in cellophane packets with a drawing of the shop and lock on the label, and sticks of pink rock with the words 'Buckby Wharf' running through the centre.

4

Willow Wren

We left Buckby Wharf with almost as much anticipation as when Pat Hayes and I set off for Braunston in 1964. Emerging on that occasion from Braunston Tunnel and descending the six locks to the Willow Wren yard, I realised fully for the first time that I was about to join that select group of men that I had admired so much when I was a boy; I was going to be a real canal boatman!

The old Grand Junction buildings by the bottom lock had been leased by Willow Wren in 1954, two years after the company had been born into a canal industry that had been in decline for over fifty years. Following World War II most of the canals, along with a large number of boats, had been nationalised, but this did nothing to reverse the downward trend and it was amid this depression that the new carrying company was formed by three men who were to become legends in the canal world. The first was Robert Aickman who, with Tom Rolt, had formed the Inland Waterways Association to fight the destruction of the canals; the second was Capt Vivian Bulkeley-Johnson, Eton and Balliol College, Oxford, a distinguished World War I army officer, Secretary of Rothchilds the bankers and honorary treasurer of the IWA; the third was Leslie Morton.

Morton had gone to sea when he was thirteen and a half, rounding Cape Horn six times under sail, and it was he, on watch as extra lookout on the starboard side of *Lusitania*'s fo'c'sle, who first saw the white trail of a torpedo arrowing towards the ship. He was one of the few survivors of the German U-boat attack which sank the ship with the loss of 1,198 passengers and crew.

Morton had been appointed general manager of the Grand Union Canal Carrying Co in 1934 and implemented an immense

12   Leslie Morton pictured at Bulls Bridge in 1965

programme of expansion which gave the company the largest fleet of long distance narrow boats ever operated. He resigned when his advocacy of further expansion was not shared by his board. His beginnings as manager of the Willow Wren Canal Carrying Co were somewhat humbler, as he later described.

On the first day of commencing operations, the total equipment consisted of a rented caravan at Paddington Basin and myself. By utilising old connections in the British Waterways, ex-Grand Union personnel, narrow boats were obtained at reasonable prices. Boatmen were engaged and carrying started within two months, with two pairs of craft. They were engaged on coal traffic from Cannock Chase to Nestles at Hayes. Within three years the fleet had risen to eight pairs, but the financial losses were steadily mounting, due principally to the old system of tolls, the poor conditions of canals and the terms of employment under which the boating families worked, which included the pernicious 'laying off money' clause (an incentive not to work).[1]

The toll system required carrying companies to pay charges on each ton of cargo and this amounted to about £180 per boat per year. Willow Wren and the Inland Waterways Association were campaigning vigorously for the replacement of this system with an annual licence costing £25 a year for each boat. 'Laying money' was paid to the boaters when they were idle through the breakdown of their boats, and many were thought by the company to take advantage of this arrangement, dubious hold ups always seeming to occur near a convenient canal-side pub.

Capt Bulkeley-Johnson provided massive sums of money over a ten year period to keep the enterprise going in the face of growing competition from road and rail, firm in his belief that the industry would flourish again. The 1962 Transport Act dissolved the British Transport Commission and on 1st January 1963 the British Waterways Board took over the administration of the inland waterways and set about reviewing the future. It was a bitter winter. For sixteen weeks all movement on the canals was frozen, and in its May 'Bulletin' the IWA reported:

> By the end of the winter, Capt Bulkeley-Johnson, who has done so much to keep the industry alive, had had enough – not, as has been suggested, of winter's cold, but of official obstruction and government indifference. He informed Mr Morton that the carrying activities of the Willow Wren Company must cease. All who love the waterways owe him a debt of gratitude for having continued so long.
>
> Mr Morton, who is prominent among the heroes which our movement has been concerned to produce and foster, has not been in the least daunted. He has evolved a new basis of operation, under which the captains of the boats will have increased personal responsibilities allied with the opportunity of increased earnings . . . By permission of Capt Bulkeley-Johnson, the new organisation is named Willow Wren Canal Transport Services Ltd . . . In the longer run, the complete success of the venture, and almost certainly the very survival of narrow boat carrying, are likely to depend upon whether or not annual licensing is introduced . . . At about the same time the new company went into action, the rumour became strong that the blue and yellow British Waterways narrow boat fleet was to be 'wasted away' within the next few months . . . if annual licensing is introduced, Mr Morton is interested in acquiring these boats also.[2]

The newly formed Board yielded to the pressure for an annual licensing scheme and decided, as the rumour had suggested they would, to discontinue the nationalised narrow boat carrying operation. Leslie Morton had campaigned for thirty years for the abolition of the old toll system and believed the concession heralded a renaissance for canal transport. He leased about forty craft from the disbanded nationalised fleet and Willow Wren took over the British Waterways traffic.

So, in 1964, Pat and I had joined a company that had won a new lease of life; there was confidence in the future of carrying on the canals and this was reflected in the bustle and activity at Willow

Wren's Braunston yard. To the right of the bottom lock, facing a row of cottages on the towpath side and dwarfing a brick shed with a slate roof (which looked more like an outside loo than the British Waterways lock keeper's office), an old dry dock, surviving from Grand Junction days, stood sentinel to the main yard below. A hump-back bridge at the tail of the lock carried a track over the cut and, peering over the parapet, one gained a bird's eye view of the company buildings huddled in a fold of shallow hills.

Working boats were tied up two and three abreast on both sides of the cut, leaving a narrow channel down the middle for passing traffic. Those on the towpath side were taking on fuel at the oil dock, once the coal store and smithy for a steam engine which pumped water from three reservoirs beside the towpath back to the summit pound. The tall, brick chimney of the pump-house could still be seen rising up behind the dock which provided diesel, paraffin and oil rags to the boaters. The diesel was stored in the boiler of the obsolete steam pump and an arm, hinged on the wall about 8ft above the ground, carried the fuel pipe and swung out across the towpath to serve the waiting boats.

There were three buildings on the right hand side, the first two of which were old brick structures. The nearest of these, stretching low along the bank, was the stores, where boaters could obtain all that was necessary to equip a pair of working narrow boats. From the depths of the gloomy interior, the slight figure of storeman Colin Clarke, brother of manager Dennis, would emerge from the dark shapes of stoves, chimneys, cans, ropes, cloths and shafts.

Standing on rails in the narrow gap between the stores and the taller workshop building, the jib of a hand-cranked crane pointed skywards with it's hook swinging menacingly over the cut like a noose. There was no adequate road access to the buildings, the narrow road (called Dark Lane) which ran down from the village turning aside rather than descending the field to the yard, so heavy items were delivered by road to the nearby Blue Line yard and taken round to Willow Wren by boat. On arrival, they were unloaded by the small crane and wheeled back along the rails to workshop and stores.

13 The view of the Willow Wren yard at Braunston as Roger saw it in 1964

14 A second shot taken from the bridge at the tail of the lock, this time 1985

Facing the canal, above the wide central door of the workshop, a wooden sign with the company's bird emblem at its centre, bore the words WILLOW WREN CANAL C CO LTD BRAUNSTON SLIPWAY BRAUNSTON PHONE 342.

Beyond the workshop, a large, white corrugated shed, recently erected, sheltered a slipway wide and deep enough to accommodate two 70ft narrow boats and inside, undergoing repairs, the long, dark form of a working boat, supported on turrets of wooden beams, could be seen with a ladder propped against its iron hull.

The boat tied nearest the bridge on this side was the butty *Cygnet*, the home of Jim Goldby, known as 'Jimpty', who was watchman at the yard. A stocky ex-miner who never married, 'Jimpty' lived with his mother until her death and he took the loss very badly. Boatman Jack Monk took him on as mate and the two men worked a pair together for years before Jack decided to marry. His wife, naturally, would work with her husband on the boats, so the redundant 'Jimpty' became caretaker at the yard.

Boats were laid up outside the workshop awaiting repairs or orders. One or two, perhaps, stood idle while someone lay ill in the cabin and, in the reservoirs beyond the yard, those making up the reserve pool of craft deteriorated slowly while waiting for gainful employment.

The Braunston yard, run as a separate company providing maintenance facilities for the carrying fleet, was Dennis Clarke's domain. Dennis's grandfather had skippered a steamer on the cut, his parents were licensees of the 'Admiral Nelson', half way down Braunston locks and Frank Nurser, whose famous boatyard had been taken over by Barlows, was his great uncle. Dennis was a skilled boat builder and painter at Barlows when, in 1954, Leslie Morton persuaded him to run Willow Wren's yard. He was revered by the boat people, who recognised his position of power and his canal pedigree, and Dennis, in turn, believed he understood the boaters.

Dennis Clarke: You weren't handling employees, you were handling families. The 'old man' would agree to something, go out and tell the 'Mrs', and you'd have the whole family in at you then, saying they weren't having it. And all the complications. I've even bailed them out of clink. I had my ups and downs with them and you'd got to stand your ground.

There were good captains and bad, but they were paid waiting money and it was the biggest mistake ever made. This industry could have got on its feet again, but the boatmen killed it. Some left the yard and you never heard anything more from them until they came in again for fuel, but the rest would break down for nothing and later you'd find out that she'd had to go to the hospital or something that day.

The first task for Pat and I when we arrived at the yard in 1964 was to ask for a butty to accompany our motor for it was imperative that, as a team of two, we should double our earning potential by working two boats. So, after finding somewhere to tie up, we went in search of Dennis Clarke. Crossing the bridge at the tail of the lock, we turned left through a gateway in a red-brick wall and stood in a muddy compound behind the old buildings. Just inside the gate on the left hand side, we found the ample Dennis squeezed into a garden shed which, with a neighbouring touring caravan, comprised Willow Wren's suite of offices.

He selected *Dabchick* from the reserve pool which was disappointing as I had hoped for a large Woolwich. This would have given maximum carrying capacity and a chance to compete on equal terms with the other pairs. His choice may have been influenced by our inexperience, or simply by the availability of boats at that time.

There was a delay while the butty, which was owned by Willow Wren and not leased from British Waterways, like *Comet*, was overhauled, so we took the opportunity to collect the additional gear we needed from the stores. We went by bus to the 'Army and Navy Stores' in Rugby and staggered back under piles of bedding and pots and pans and the miscellany of things we needed to set up home.

After what seemed an interminable wait, but was actually a week, *Dabchick* was ready and *Comet*, still wearing her plain and shabby British Waterways blue, was shamed by the butty's freshly painted Willow Wren livery. The large green panels on her cabin sides were bordered with cream and carried the company's name in cream lettering. There was a big red disc in the centre of each panel, again edged in cream, and the smaller rear panels contained traditionally painted castles. This three colour scheme was continued along the top plank, which carried the boat's name, to the rudder and tiller.

On a pair of narrow boats with similar dimensions, the absence of gunnels on the butty makes its cabin a few precious inches wider than the cabin on the motor and preferable, therefore, as living accommodation; so Pat and I moved the big old range from *Dabchick*'s cabin into *Comet* and replaced it with the more convenient Calor Gas model and a small solid fuel fire for heating. Then we distributed our new acquisitions about the butty's marginally wider, though still tiny cabin, content in the knowledge that the intimacy it imposed would compensate for any lack of space, and waited for our orders.

At first glance, the view from the bridge at the bottom lock had changed little in twenty one years. The same buildings stood on either side of the canal and boats still jostled for space in the water. However, a closer look revealed changes in the scene. The old working boats, both functional and pleasing to the eye, were outnumbered by modern steel narrow boat cruisers, a species unborn in the mid-sixties and, for the most part, short, straight and graceless by comparison. But there were exceptions, for some fine traditional style boats are now built at Braunston.

Willow Wren gave up the lease to the yard in 1968 and it was assigned by British Waterways to Chris Barney's Braunston Boats Ltd. Chris was a civil engineer who saw scope for building boats for both commercial and pleasure purposes. He came down from Gas Street aboard the old wooden Shropshire Union boat *Silver Jubilee*, which he had refurbished as a houseboat, and tied up at the wharf. The yard was derelict and overrun by brambles, with heaps of bricks and rubble everywhere and the remaining buildings in very poor shape. Chris cleared the site with a bulldozer and with the meagre experience gained from restoring *Silver Jubilee*, began repairing and building boats.

Willow Wren continued to operate a small fleet of working boats and Braunston Boats fuelled and serviced them and distributed the boatmen's wages. Ex-Willow Wren man Stan Argent was taken on, with his old employers contributing to his keep in return for his acting as their representative at the yard. Quite a lot of repair work was undertaken on the carrying boats, including British Waterways craft that were being sold off at the time, and two new boats were built in the first year.

Chris Barney: The big asbestos shed built by Willow Wren had an earth floor and there were two ordinary crab winches at the back, concreted in rather inadequately, for pulling the boats up sideways. Two concrete runways, perpendicular to the canal side and about 4ft wide, ran to the water. You laid the boat on heavy beams and slid it down into the cut, but unlike properly built slipways, there was a sheer drop at the water's edge. You didn't pull the boats straight up the slipways, you sort of heaved them over the edge and it was extremely dangerous. The first boat we pulled up, I think, was *Kimberley*, the old *Enterprise* passenger boat from Reading, which we re-bottomed.

Only a few wooden boats had been purpose built for the infant canal leisure industry. When Chris began, one or two enterprising companies were starting to build the odd steel hulled boat and before very long everyone was jumping on the band-wagon, turning them out on a production line basis.

The biggest visible change at the yard was the large mooring basin which was excavated at the end of the slipway in 1975. A new railed slip, this time plunging deep into the basin, allowed craft to be winched out safely, bows first, through an opening in the side of the corrugated shed. At that time boats had been singled out for a higher level of v.a.t. fixed at 25 per cent, putting rather a damper on sales. So Chris applied to British Waterways for hire licences and his small fleet of holiday craft shared the basin with a diversity of private boats and some real narrow boats. The old work horses

15 Chris Barney on the wharf at Braunston

had survived in surprisingly large numbers at Braunston due, particularly, to the presence of a fleet of camping boats run from the old oil dock opposite, by Union Canal Carriers.

The story of UCC is the story of Janusz Rokicki, who came to England from Poland in 1946. From then on, the significant dates of his absorption into the world of canals broadly correspond with my own. It was in 1957, while working as a jeweller in London's Hatton Garden, that he and his wife Ruth took their first canal holiday. They were fascinated by the cut and bought their first narrow boat, the former Grand Union motor *Bexhill*, from BWB in 1964. A couple of years later, Janusz put in sealed tenders for several redundant 'Waterways' boats, hoping to secure one of them. He was offered the lot, so set up Foxton Boat Services with Robin Hewitt and Tony Matts.

The company moved to Braunston in 1970, employing several ex-boaters on winter carrying, but when the cargoes dried up they concentrated on operating the fleet as camping boats during the summer months. Turn-round days would see Janusz surrounded by excited children, and cardboard boxes full of baked bean cans, bottles of washing-up liquid, and toilet rolls. In 1982, while they were on holiday at Ironbridge, Ruth and Janusz were killed by a runaway lorry. But for them, fewer working boats would grace the canal at Braunston.

The second alteration one noticed, was the transformation of the old stores into a modern chandlery. Chris Barney had continued to use the building as a store for his boat building business, with a small retail trade in cotton lines, nuts and bolts and other boating essentials. Later, it became a fascinating shop selling canal bric-à-brac; old books long out of print, lace plates, glass shades for oil lamps, Measham tea pots, cans and stools painted by the old boatyard pros, ranges and rope fenders filled the dim and musty old building.

Then, during the winter of 1979–80, British Waterways dredged along the wharf. Silt coming down from the lock had reduced the depth of water to about 2ft; but dredging increased this to 6ft and, for the first time in many years, boats could get right into the side. But two years later, tell-tale cracks appeared in the store wall nearest the canal. The precious stock was hastily evacuated and the roof was propped up, just before the stone coping shoring the canal bank, closely followed by the store wall, fell into the cut. It has been suggested that British Waterways consistently lowered the water level by a foot to avoid the risk of weekend flooding and, as a consequence, frost got down behind the coping, where the ground was very wet, and dislodged it. Chris reverted to selling odds and ends from the back of the propped up building, with customers clambering over the rubble to get in, but now the store had been rebuilt in conjunction with Midland Chandlers and stocked a wide range of equipment for the modern boater.

So there had been changes, but the ghost of Willow Wren haunted the place. The 'green hut', used as an office by Dennis Clarke, still stood inside the gateway, though now it was painted white, and the aged caravan had been relegated to a corner of the yard along with the little crane. The old sign board hanging on the workshop wall read: 'Braunston Boats Ltd', but its weathered and peeling paint was like a disintegrating shroud, falling away to reveal the faded lettering of the Willow Wren original.

A little further along the cut, where two elegant cast iron bridges span the diverging waterways at Braunston Junction, the far from ghostly Dennis Clarke looked just as he did in the sixties. Continuing to ease his stout frame into spaces the size of narrow boat cabins, Dennis conducts the business of the trip boat *Water Ouzel* from another tiny office at the back of the sort of hut one might see on a village cricket field and hear described rather exaggeratedly as 'the pavilion'. Willow Wren started in the hire business in 1964 and George Walker, who founded Swan Line at Fradley seven years earlier, joined the company, taking over the running of *Water Ouzel*. The boat, a Star Class little Woolwich originally called *Sun*, was built for the Grand Union company in 1935 and it was George's pride and joy. Dennis, who had been running the Willow Wren hire fleet and hotel boats from Rugby, took over the tripper when George died in 1984 and observes the cut with amusement from his vantage point at what must surely be the busiest junction on the entire canal network.

Dennis Clarke: We would come out of Nurser's yard and we'd never see another boat, except for the odd one at the depot, all the way round to Calcutt and back. Now, on Saturday evenings in the summer, all the hire boats that come out from Rugby, Weltonfields and Weedon get down here about the same time. It's chaos! You can see twelve boats wedged around the island and when you leave the wharf and get round the corner going towards Buckby, you can't drive your boat until you're out of the locks because they are moored every inch of the way.

Hire boats were certainly scarce in 1964, when Dennis despatched our ill-matched pair to Hawkesbury Junction, where the traffic control office would direct us to one of the pits for loading; but in 1985, we approached the first bridge hole after Braunston Turn just as a hirer closed in from the opposite direction. The lady steerer ploughed determinedly for the gap until, realising that we were nearer and had precedence, she panicked and yelled for help. Her startled husband emerged from below, but his frantic efforts to avoid a collision were seriously impaired by his wrestling with the zip on his trousers, and it was too late. It was an amusing incident, with only egos damaged, but I took it, and the scars on the next bridge, as a warning to be alert to such dangers when we set off with the loaded boats.

16   Dennis Clarke

5

Loading at Hawkesbury

As we approached Hawkesbury, or Sutton Stop as it is known by the boaters, the countryside gave way to a housing estate, road haulage premises (much tidier than they used to be despite the presence of one or two old lorries rusting in the yard) and electricity pylons. By the cut on the right hand side, we passed an expanse of waste ground with tall grass pushing up through the black earth. In the sixties, mountains of coal were stock-piled here, but now the area was flat and empty, for Hawkesbury Power Station was in the process of being demolished and the conveyor which carried the coal across the cut had gone. Steel girders stuck out of the gutted building like bones and part of the roof had collapsed and sagged to the ground at one end, looking uncannily like the arched back and tail of a great, beached whale.

Next door, Coventry Sub Station was very much alive. Pylons strode in from all directions and rows of live electric conductors, resembling giant spark plugs, hummed and buzzed, fortified by a spiked fence festooned with warning notices: 275,000 VOLTS. SAFETY HELMETS MUST BE WORN. DANGER!

The familiar engine house chimney was in sight as we came around the last bend to the Stop. We worked through the stop lock and eased under the iron bridge spanning the junction, turning left onto the Coventry Canal. *Comet* had not arrived, so we made *Barnes* secure at the wharf opposite the colliery cottages, where we would load from lorries on the following day, and set off to explore the canal into the city.

Unusually, the water in the cut was crystal clear, and it was possible to see what is normally concealed by murky brown liquid. I counted, among the other rubbish, two tractor tyres, countless wooden palets, plastic bollards, milk crates, a sofa and two arm-chairs (the same suite), masses of polystyrene and polythene and a rusted Mini!

The stand roofs and floodlights of the football ground rose out of a mass of two-up, two-down terraces and an elegant row of red-brick houses with large windows along the top storey – Cash's Hundred Houses – looked impressive after their recent resto-ration. They were built by Joseph Cash in 1857 (48 were actually completed, of which 37 remain) at a time when people weaving in their own homes were unable to compete with the factories' power-driven looms. A firm believer in the value of cottage indus-try, Joseph gave his workers the best of both worlds, installing a steam engine in the courtyard which powered the looms in the light, airy workshops at the tops of the houses. Apparently, at the first whistle each day, each man climbed through a trap-door to his workshop and stood ready by his loom; at a second whistle, the power was turned on and he began weaving.

The houses have been split now, into two. The ground and first floors have been modernised and the top shops converted into flats, with access via newly constructed sections, supposedly in keeping with the original design. In reality, the new bits stick out like sore thumbs.

After turning in the sadly neglected Coventry Basin, we re-turned to Hawkesbury to find *Comet* tied inside *Barnes* and all the gear from her hold neatly laid out on the wharf in front of the boatmen's wash house. The top planks, placed one on top of the other, and the long and short shafts laid beside them, were painted in red oxide gloss. Lines of differing lengths and thicknesses such as snubbers, snatchers, cross straps and strings, each used to execute a specific boating task, were individually coiled. The big green top cloths were neatly folded and a rope bow fender encased in a section of rubber tyre. A shovel completed the group, leaving *Comet*'s clean-swept hold ready to receive its cargo of coal. Ian, characteristically, was mopping down the counter and cabin. He thrust the cloth mop head into the cut, then spun the 'barber's pole' shaft expertly in his arms to expel the excess water, the flying droplets prescribing a perfect circle in the air. Looking up, he greeted us with his usual nod and half smile.

Hawkesbury was a sombre place as we made *Barnes* ready in heavy rain, stashing odds and ends under the cratch and fiddling around doing insignificant last minute jobs. One or two narrow boat cruisers braved the downpour, the bright orange kagools and life jackets of their crews brilliant against the stormy sky, and an old couple with two bedraggled little dogs sheltered under the canopy of the wash-house. The old lady trudged forlornly round the building in search of a public toilet, trying all the locked doors. Built, originally, for the benefit of the working boaters, who could use the baths and washing machines to clean up after loading at the nearby collieries, the building had been refurbished as a sanitary station for pleasure boaters, with the original structure remaining inside a new shell. Entry, alas, can only be gained with a British Waterways key.

As the rain eased, two magnificent rainbows graced the dark grey sky and the white frontage and chimneys of the 'Greyhound', and the wet, red roof tiles, shone in the evening sunlight shafting through the breaking cloud. An old man, who had been watching our labours from the iron bridge which crossed the junction, ambled down the slope towards us, his flat cap at a jaunty angle and his hands shoved deep into the pockets of his trousers, which were supported by both braces and a wide leather belt buckled behind his back.

He said his name was Carter and that he had been on the Ovaltine boats, and as he spoke, the rolled dog-end in his mouth stuck disconcertingly to his bottom lip.[1] Mr Carter pulled a wallet from the inside pocket of his jacket and took out some pictures of his boats. One showed a blond, curly haired little boy peering over the back deck of a butty. The family, he said, had left the cut in 1954 in order that his son, who by then was eight, could go to school. Now the boy was a lorry driver and Mr Carter lived at Hawkesbury and was a regular at the 'Greyhound'.

We followed the old man over to the pub and into the back bar, where he joined his cronies who were playing dominoes at a row of tables at the far end. They could have been sitting among the simple wooden tables and chairs in this unadorned room ever

17 (above)
Charlie Carter,
Ovaltine
boatman and,
18 (right) The
young Ted
Ward,
pictured in the
early sixties.
He carried
Willow Wren's
last load

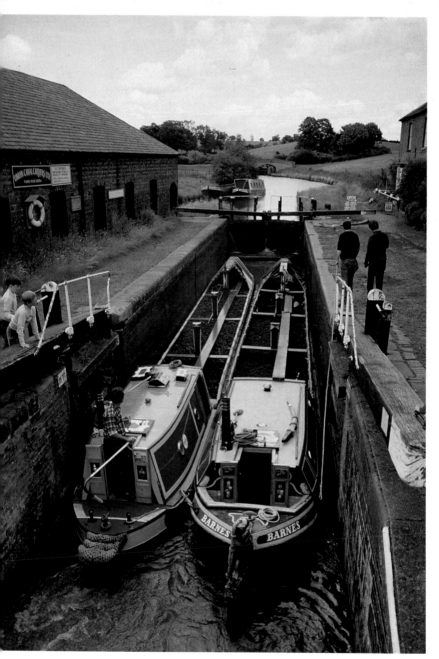

In the bottom lock at Braunston – the dry-dock on the left

2   *Comet* in 1964 showing signs of wear and tear and *Dabchick*, crewed by Roger Alsop and Patricia Hayes

Loading at Sutton Stop

4   Ian Kemp steering *Comet*, the open cabin doors, '. . . bright
yellow in the evening sun'

since I last walked out in 1965, for the scene was just as I remembered it. At the small bar, a group of men and women chattered and laughed noisily, among them a voluble young man named John Forth, who is John Yates' Midlands counterpart, selling house coal from his single motor *Newbury*. But the similarity between the two goes no further than the selling of coal along the cut, for John Yates is fair, well-spoken and unable to disguise a certain schoolboy awkwardness. Forth is much shorter, a cast in one of his bright eyes and his full, dark beard making him resemble a mischievous pirate. Holding court at the bar of the 'Greyhound', he heartily ridiculed those who 'play at narrow boat carrying, loading a few tons and calling it boating'. John Yates is more guarded with his criticism, managing to find something meritorious in everyone's efforts.

John Forth gave up a tedious factory job to buy a working boat from one such enthusiast who quickly lost his enthusiasm, and carries on his business full time, living and working permanently on his boat. He is, consequently, a pragmatist, preferring a recently built steel boat, which is easily maintained, to an old one more acceptable to the traditionalists. He plans to buy a butty and extend the cabin to accommodate a shower as all his friends who live in houses, he says, are fed up with him and his wife continually cadging baths. John Yates, readily conceding that he enjoys the advantage of being able to return to the relative luxury of his full length conversion at Battlebridge after a trip, says he's soft, but the two men share a mutual respect, each acknowledging that his rival is serious about his occupation on the cut. I wondered what the old boys in the corner thought.

Many other ex-boaters live in the area. Ted and Ann Ward and their daughter Julie moved into a council house at nearby Henley Green after carrying Willow Wren's last load in August 1970. A boat cabin stool, painted in the traditional manner, stands in the living room and the ornaments on the big colour television are a brass exhaust pipe and oil pressure gauge, precious mementoes from their boats.

Ted Ward: Bulls Bridge made that stool for me when I was at

British Waterways and I painted it. I kept the brass pipe and the oil gauge and I've got windlasses upstairs. I wouldn't part with anything like that. My parents worked for Fellows, Morton & Clayton and their parents worked on the horse boats. All me relations worked on the boats and I had my own pair at seventeen. When I first started on my own, there was a gaffer called Ted Wood in charge of the British Waterways fleet who said to me: 'You can have this pair of boats to navigate, or you can have them to decorate; but I tell you one thing, you don't get no money for the decorating! I never knowed them boats to be any longer than three days from London to Birnigum and I don't want to hear any excuses now'.

When it packed up I went to the Rugby Portland Cement Co doing shift work. It was a wrench and it seemed strange knowing you was greased up there for eight hours a day. You worked sixteen or eighteen hours on a boat, there was always something happening different and you didn't get bored. I still can't sleep after three in the morning.

I heard the first lorry draw up at a quarter to seven and as I stuck my head out of the hatch, it started to rain again. This first load was 20 tonnes of small, almond shaped nuts called Maxibrite, which had come all the way from Pontyclun, Mid Glamorgan. John chooses to load at Sutton Stop because it is close to the south Warwickshire pits and is, therefore, in a low price zone; but the National Coal Board can supply coal from any pit they choose and deliveries may come from one of the large, low cost pits in Nottinghamshire or Yorkshire or, as in this case, from south Wales.

I had never loaded from lorries during my time with Willow Wren, so Ian, who had done so many times while working *Comet* for Stroudwater Carriers, took charge of proceedings. It had simply been a matter, he said, of releasing the tail board and trying desperately to control the torrent of coal by continually dropping and lifting the body of the lorry. This time, however, there was a small square opening, with a slide, in the centre of the tail board which allowed a great deal more control over the flow of coal.

19 (left) Ted Ward at home in Coventry, 1985 and 20 (below) Loading at Sutton Stop

We didn't know exactly how much coal John had ordered for this particular trip, the final amount depending, one assumes, on his order book; so, expecting that the second delivery might be slightly less than 20 tonnes, we decided to load the butty, which had the greater capacity and the lesser draught, first. The lorry tipped up and I opened the slide. Nothing happened, so I jabbed at the coal with my shovel and it started pouring through the gap, drumming onto the boards in the bottom of the hold. Even through the smaller opening the flow could be too swift, so Ian shouted to the driver to lower the body and by doing this, and moving the boat along, we managed to distribute the load pretty evenly.

It was desirable to be a little bow heavy, as too much weight at the stern would make going aground more likely, but a hard look showed that she was a little too far down at the head. So, with two shovels, and a wheelbarrow borrowed from a workshop behind the 'Greyhound', we shifted a quantity from bow to stern until the load was properly trimmed and we were satisfied that the butty would swim nicely when underway. We rolled the side cloths down tightly and tied the strings; laid the planks end to end, from the cabin top forward onto each of the cross beams, forming a walk-way along the length of the hold; mopped away the slimy, wet coal dust which covered everything, and waited for the second lorry.

As we sheltered under the canopy of the wash-house, a van arrived and three workmen, donning yellow waterproofs, trundled out a motor mower. In 1976, 'Because of its unique character, and its historical associations with the early years of the industrial revolution and the development of the canal system', Coventry City Council and Nuneaton Borough Council designated the Junction, which straddles the boundary between the two local authorities, a conservation area hence the grass cutting gang.[2] All was tidy, with benches, litter bins and 'rustic' fencing springing up along with the young trees and new grass. Buildings had been restored and structures refurbished but, inevitably, the 'unique character' referred to in the official brochure, had been lost.

Hawkesbury was an altogether scruffier place, saturated in the stink from the adjacent Courtaulds tip when Pat and I moored *Comet* and *Dabchick* with the other Willow Wren pairs above the stop lock in 1964. Here was the Willow Wren boats' place in the Stop's pecking order. The immaculate Blue Line boats, descended from the old Barlows fleet, held pride of place with the Whitlock's pair *Ian* and *Lucy* tied abreast outside the 'Greyhound' and the Bray's *Roger* and *Raymond* just in front of them. The remnants of British Waterways' disbanded fleet lined the Coventry Canal opposite, stretching halfway to Bedworth. Smoke curled from the chimneys of about thirty pairs of idle blue and yellow boats. Set out in their sheeted over holds were tables and chairs and shabby three piece suites and above, suspended between shafts that jutted into the air, lines of washing flapped dismally.

The Board were negotiating at the time with a number of local councils to find housing for their redundant boatmen and meantime the families continued to live on their boats, making the most of the extra space offered by empty holds. These boatmen worked 'on the bank', or scratched their mark each week on the Labour Exchange docket. They had rejected the offer, taken up by many of their fellows, of working for Willow Wren. Perhaps they were shy of piece-work and the scrapping of 'laying money', or was it, simply, that they no longer saw a future on the cut?

Among the Willow Wren people gathered above the stop lock was Ray White, the young boatman we had met on the Stratford Canal. Ray, like Pat and myself, was 'off the land' and did not belong to one of the old canal families; consequently, he showed none of the boaters' reserve towards newcomers. Since joining Willow Wren, I had felt keenly the boat people's reticence and was dismayed by stories about their hostility. 'They will not accept you', I was told. 'Turn your back on them and they will drop you with a windlass'. It was all inconsistent with the congenial relationships I had enjoyed with the boaters when I was a lad and during my hotel boating days. But I had not presumed then to be a member of their club and suddenly, I doubted if I should have applied.

21 The tail-end of the 'dead' British Waterways fleet. In 1985, *Comet* and *Barnes* loaded exactly where *Bodmin* is tied up

Ray showed us how best to negotiate the infamous Hawkesbury hairpin, a manageable turn with empty boats, but a daunting proposition when fully loaded, and my doubts grew. The more experienced man pointed out the correct position and speed of approach and suggested a technique which would avoid having to jump ashore with a rope to pull the fore end around the turn. 'Everyone will be watching', said Ray, 'and if you get it wrong, the motor will end up in Braunston while the butty makes for Coventry'. One or two of the 'old school', like the Whitlocks, used a line to assist them, probably a throw-back to horse boating practice, but it was a matter of honour for everyone to accomplish the manoeuvre with style.

Ted Ward: They all used to be packed into the 'Greyhound' on a dinner time and they used to watch you come round, see how good you did compared with them and if there was a load of people watching, you could guarantee something 'ud go wrong. One day one of my brothers was in the pub and he was cocking a glass of beer up as if to say, 'Are you going to come in and get it with the boat?' They used to be insulting like that. You needed all the bend to get two boats round. They would just miss the wall and go round lovely.

Ray directed me to the traffic office, a small red brick building standing on the piece of land sandwiched by the converging waterways. Inside, the lady who issued the orders handed me a slip of paper. She must have taken pity on us, for we were to go to Newdigate, the nearest of the three collieries served by Willow Wren on the Coventry Canal, the others being Baddesley and Pooley Hall.

At noon, unable to contain our frustration any longer after hours of cowering under the canopy of the wash-house, sipping endless mugs of steaming coffee and tea and peering out gloomily at the incessant rain, I braved the elements and dashed across the car park to the canal shop next to the 'Greyhound' and rang John Yates in London. He advised patience, but knowing it was the last available day for loading before the pits broke up for their annual holiday, it was difficult not to be anxious.

To ease the tension, I decided to walk the mile or so up the towpath to Newdigate. Where the line of 'dead' British Waterways boats had begun, I passed an old butty called *Dipper*, nicely painted in the same blue and yellow livery, piled high with rusting car bodies, engine blocks and gas cookers. Towing this fascinating pile of junk around the waterways with a scruffy narrow boat cruiser, a short, stocky, friendly man with fair curls, a Romany nose and dangling ear-ring, wheels and deals in scrap.

A submerged butty in the Newdigate Arm's stagnant water pointed the way to the derelict colliery wharf, which is approached through a rectangular bridge hole. Above, the Coventry to Nuneaton railway crosses the cut on a flat concrete span, supported by blue brick abutments daubed with graffiti. Beyond the bridge, the steel skeleton of a large shed, which was moved back and forth on rails to keep the coal from getting wet during loading, rusted on the concrete wharf, and a second sunken hulk stuck up out of the water, its broken and rotting wooden hull choked with weed. Except for the singing of birds and the distant barking of a dog, the place was silent and still.

In the old days, I never saw the pit beyond the wharf, and now it was too late, for Newdigate Colliery closed down in 1982 and the grassy slopes of the Miners' Welfare Park camouflage the old workings. What I did see in 1964, was a steam engine at the top of a steep incline, pushing three big coal trucks which were uncoupled and free-wheeled down the slope. They trundled along the track set into the wharf and rolled into the shed, where the brake-man brought them to a halt by the waiting narrow boats. Two pairs were permitted in the arm at any one time and the crews helped each other with the loading. The truck sides facing the boats were dropped down and a chute clipped into position; then you climbed into the truck and shovelled the coal into the chute, from where it tumbled into the boats.

When the first three trucks had been laboriously emptied, the engine returned and with much clanking, shunted them back up the slope to fetch another three full ones for the next pair. It was an unpopular trip among the boaters because the coal was in the form

22 The derelict colliery wharf at Newdigate

of fine dust which permeated into the cabins and settled in the skin and hair and clothes. It was necessary, also, to sheet up the boats to protect the offensive cargo for, if it got wet in transit, they would not allow you to unload it until it had dried out and precious time and money would be lost.

We turned out of the Newdigate Arm on 23rd July 1964, carrying 49 tons 11 cwt, for delivery to the West Herts Drainage Board's Colne Valley Sewage works at Rickmansworth. I was dismayed at the extra effort needed to manoeuvre the loaded boats, which seemed to have acquired a mind of their own, and we immediately thudded into the bank. My trepidation mounted by the minute as we approached the hairpin at Hawkesbury and the moment of truth came all too soon. Passing through the narrow before the bend, I slowed the motor and allowed the butty to gain as I steered into the position of approach that Ray had described and sensed the eyes steadily watching my every move. I pushed the tiller hard over to make the turn, then thrust the engine into reverse and *Dabchick*, coming up behind, hit the motor's counter stern, spinning her bow around the bend. Then I was moving forward again and Pat, rowing furiously with the butty tiller, brought *Dabchick* inching and straining round behind. I looked back at my mate, whose relief was obvious and matched my own mounting elation and beyond, I watched the boaters turn away unmoved and go about their business.

The second, very impressive lorry, with its gleaming yellow cab and aluminium body, finally turned up at three, this time from Rotherham, with 22 tonnes of washed cobbles; we had guessed wrongly and the motor would be carrying more than the butty, which would look unprofessional. Ian slipped black plastic bin liners over the stands to protect the paint work and loading commenced in bright sunshine.

We set off at a quarter to six and immediately hit trouble. As *Comet*'s stern end swung out to the far bank to make the turn, a piece of carpet wound itself around the prop, an unwanted complication which made an already awkward manoeuvre even more difficult. This time the spectators were idle and inexpert, but even they looked unimpressed with our efforts.

The tattered remnants of the offending rug were prized off in the stop lock and I settled down to steering the butty. Although I had not steered *Barnes* in the old days I had taken a turn with *Dabchick*, but I had almost forgotten the serenity derived from the gently swaying motion and the sound of water lazily lapping the piled banks. An old man, bending to his work in a potato field, bobbed up like a startled rabbit as we passed; people hurried down to the canal to catch a glimpse of us; unusually amiable anglers remarked on how many years it had been since they last saw a working pair; and boaters dived below for their cameras.

It was a beautiful evening, almost too good to be true. As we left the electricity pylons and the M6 behind, the fresh wind dropped to nothing, birds sang, and church bells rang out across the wheatfields past Ansty, which were darkened by the long, slanting shadows of the trees. Then we moved along an embankment with the railway a step higher on our left. I remembered steam trains along here, but now the Inter City diesels thundered by and you could feel the boat bump with the vibration as they passed. To our right, an airship and a plane glinted in a pale yellow sky over the distant Coventry skyline, which was punctuated by high-rise buildings and tall chimneys, church spires and the floodlight pylons of Coventry City football ground.

We approached Newbold down the long cutting at about eleven. It was very dark, with the overhanging trees screening any light from the clear night sky. *Comet*'s headlight thrust forward into the gloom and Ian and the cabin chimney were silhouetted against the arc of light. Dozens of luminous green points sprinkled the banks like tiny cats' eyes, showing the way for the unlighted butty; were they glow worms, or the isotopes that anglers attach to their floats for night fishing?

At the far end of Newbold Tunnel, the engine relaxed as the motor neared the inevitable line of moored boats, and heads peered inquisitively round curtains and bobbed up in hatches as it passed. Our stealthy approach went almost unnoticed and we slid silently up in the dark, listening to the naive and charming comments about the 'coal barges'.

23 Loaded and ready to go

24 Making the turn at Hawkesbury, carpet and all

6

Boaters and Boating

We left Newbold at half past seven, heading east, each with a hand clasped to his forehead, shielding our eyes against the low morning sun, and very soon passed the arm leading to Rugby Wharf. It was here, soon after the reformation of the carrying company in 1963, that Willow Wren began in the hire business. The enterprise, under the management of George Walker, started with boats bought from the carrying fleet. Under a plastic sheet in a field at the end of the arm, the old wooden Joshers *Kingfisher*, *Shoveller* and *Wagtail* were sawn in half and converted into hire craft.

As we approached the first of the three locks at Hillmorton, I heard a shout and turning, expected to see a girl on a rusty old bicycle. But that was 1964! She had caught us up on that first trip, riding hard along the towpath to set the locks for a pair of following boats and seeing that Pat and I were newcomers, she shouted across, 'Pull over and let us pass'. I looked behind, but her boats, which would have stolen our 'road' if I allowed them to go by, were not in sight. 'I'll let your pair through when they're at the back of my boats and not until', I bellowed back. The same request was repeated often during the following weeks by diminutive 'lock wheelers' and acted as an incentive for us to work hard to try to stay ahead.

However, my assertiveness deserted me at Rowington, on our second trip. The long Hatton flight was continually drawing water from this particular pound, and with the level down by a foot, a pair of boats up ahead of us had run aground in the middle of the cut. Their elderly steerer signalled to me to stop and this time I felt obliged to obey, for he stood suspiciously eyeing the narrow gap between boat and bank, shook his head gravely and said that we would never get through. During the day and a half that we waited for the British Waterways tug to come and pull him off, I sat and contemplated countless boats approach from the opposite direction and squeeze through the shallow gap, but I couldn't, for some unknown reason that baffles me still, bring myself to defy the old man's advice and try to take my own pair through.

There are three pairs of single locks at Hillmorton and they provided the first real opportunity to oil our rusty techniques. Ian cast the butty adrift approaching the first pair, moved into his lock and left *Comet* in forward gear against the top gate; *Barnes* sailed sedately into hers and the mast line was made fast to the top paddle post. When both locks were full and the gates open, the butty was snatched out on a long line and we were away in fine style. But pride comes before a fall.

Adopting the usual working practice, we rounded the bend leading to the second pair in the flight on the outside, only to find that there was not enough water. In the old days one could normally rely on a depth of 4ft on the outside of bends due to the continual passage of working boats, but now, with no working craft and shallow draughted pleasure boats constantly cutting off corners, there was no deep channel. The grounded motor was refloated by flushing water through the right hand lock, which looked strangely nude without its accompanying cottage. When the old building disappeared under a Rugby Borough Council demolition order, the problem of disposing of the rubble was solved by the Warwickshire Fly Boat Co who moved it in narrow boats to their base at Stockton, where the hardcore forms the base of a new dry dock.

We came towards Braunston, with the church spire dominating the landscape, and the new housing estate bestriding the hill formed a back cloth for a tense little drama unfolding in a field by the cut. A man watched his lurcher in headlong pursuit of a rabbit which skidded under a gate and disappeared round a hedge on the other side, running for its life. The big dog lost a vital second or two wriggling through the bars and then took up the chase. Twenty years ago, the man could well have been a boatman, for

25 Working through a pair of the single locks at Hillmorton

26 Arthur and Ernie, with Ernie's young son, watch the boats go by. Note the wooden disc on the mooring rope – to stop rats climbing aboard!

poaching, and scrumping, were considered legitimate means of obtaining food.

Arthur and Ernie had heard us coming and as *Comet* drew nearer, I could see Ernie beckoning to the old man, who was hurrying along the towpath. As I passed the bow of their boat *Poacher*(!) Ernie called out, 'How's it going?' and they stood watching until the boats were out of site. Arthur and Rose Bray, with Rose's son Ernie Kendall, had worked for the elite Blue Line Canal Carriers, who took over the Braunston yard and carrying fleet of the old established Samuel Barlow Coal Co in 1962. Of all the boaters in the sixties, it was they who made the biggest impression on me. They were strange, somehow, and I was in awe of them. Their boats, *Roger* and *Raymond*, in common with the other Blue Line pairs, were always immaculate and they worked, with wonderful efficiency, what appeared to be seven days a week round the clock shifts.

They passed us once as we both made for Baddesley to load coal and were returning fully laden before we had reached the wharf. We loaded and set off in pursuit, but had not progressed very far before their resplendent pair bore down on us again, coming back empty for their next load.

Ernie Kendall: Yes, we was the best. There used to be us and Mr Whitlock. They're related to us. We used to keep going up and down. When you're on trading boats you're doing seven days a week; if you load on a Friday you see and you're back, and you load again on a Friday, you got no weekends off like you are now. And we never counted the hours. It was about eighty six I should think on the journey right around, the time as you worked it out.

We admired them immensely, but the rivalry between the families was intense and there were no holds barred on the cut.

Ted Ward: The Brays and the Whitlocks ran one way to the jam factory and unloaded, but we used to load a boat two roads and you was doing better than them. They used to say,

27   'Yes, we was the best'. The Brays at work in the 60s

'Oh, we done that trip in a week', and I'd say, 'That's nothing to be proud on 'cause we done two trips in eight days and there's lesser people working our boats'. We worked from four in the morning till ten at night. You went to the pub with your own people and you was friends, but once you left you got on with your work, it was *your* business. There was a lot of aggro and I haven't got so many friends now.

At the end of September 1970, the Blue Line boats carried their last loads to the 'Jam 'Ole'. Arthur, who was due to draw his pension in the December, retired. Ernie got a maintenance job with the Waterways and they lived aboard their butty *Raymond* at the entrance to the Blue Line yard. Rose died in 1971 and later Ernie married and bought *Poacher*, a Hancock & Lane hull fitted out by Dennis Clarke. They are suspicious of strangers though Ernie, with a deep voice resonating from his stocky frame, can be expansive in company he trusts. He wears a woolly hat, a collar and tie and regulation British Waterways overalls. Arthur is taller, with a slight stoop, his quiet speech a little slurred after a stroke, but his small, deep set eyes ever watchful under the brim of his old brown trilby.

Acquiring *Poacher* has given them back their mobility (they recently returned to the 'Jam 'Ole' for the first time since carrying finished) and revived their main topic of conversation (ie. how quickly they boated from here, to there, and back again, despite the odds).

Ernie Kendall: You see, there's too many pleasure boats about and *they* tell *us* what to do. You got to keep waiting at every lock for 'em. If you get by one boat at one lock, you'll be waiting at the next, the same thing over and over. If we was a going from here, how far would we get in a day? You wouldn't get above Stoke Bruerne. I mean, Stoke Bruerne 'ud be no good to us, we should want to be up about Leighton Buzzard or somewhere from here, and then down nearly to Southall. You couldn't make a living on it now.

28 Those most respected boaters, the Brays in 1985

29   Roger with George Phipps

Making a living on it was the priority for the handful of us who came 'off the land' in the sixties; that, and to be taken seriously by such people as the Brays. We had to earn their respect. Pat and I repeated two or three times our feat at Hawkesbury turn, wringing the odd, barely discernable nod of approval from the attendant boaters. Word spread along the canal grapevine and, gradually, we noticed signs of a thaw in their antagonism. Someone showed us how to load timber into the boats and someone else warned that our cratch[1] would not go under a certain bridge. Through these brief exchanges, we got to know the Harrisons and the Collins, the Smiths, Humphreys, Beecheys and Hunts. They delighted in demonstrating their know-how and I, for my part, was thankful that I hadn't had to ask, for I knew that if ever I admitted that there was something I couldn't do, I would be ridiculed and quickly lose what little respect I had managed to win.

Ted Ward: I used to think it was funny. We knowed how to load a boat so it would go along the water fast, but they would do just the opposite. I never give anybody any tips 'cause I never got teached meself; they had to earn your respect and if they stuck it out and got better, then we tormented them a bit more. Some, like Ray White, spent quite a few years on the boats, but he never got passed out as a boat person. Unless its in your blood, your family had been in it for generations, you never got accepted. People say to me, 'What do you have to do to make one?' but you can't you see.

Our hard won, but fragile, respectability was soon put to the test. I was still concerned about *Dabchick*'s limited carrying capacity and the fact that the butty was leaking badly gave me an opportunity to do something about it. I reported the boat's deteriorating condition to Dennis Clarke, who suggested we take *Barnes*, which was due to resume service after docking at Braunston. I was pleased to be given a big boat at last, but there was a snag.

Barnes had originally been allocated to George Phipps and his family who were on their way to collect it. The company now considered my claim more pressing, but said I must be willing to face the consequences of taking a boat which George considered his. I wanted the boat, but knew that if I took it there was likely to be, at the very least, some ill feeling. When I decided to go ahead, word spread quickly and the Willow Wren staff sadistically predicted the outcome. 'George is on his way and God help you'. 'He'll really sort you out'. 'I wouldn't be in your shoes mate'.

The Phipps family were justly famous on the cut for their tea. They would begin a pot on Monday morning, adding boiling water and more tea to the vast, steaming receptacle throughout the week. All and sundry would get a cup until it was finally emptied of its evil contents on Sunday night, ready for the whole process to begin again.

George and his wife had a young son and two teenage daughters. Pat had given clothes to the girls and helped them with sewing and mending, and I considered George and myself to be friends. But now, setting off from Braunston with the big butty, we knew that we would meet the family within five or six miles and we wondered how they would react. In the end, they just ignored us. George was obviously very hurt about the whole thing, but we had a living to make and we wanted to do it properly, there was no point in going round with half a load. The other boaters recognised our claim to the boat and there were no recriminations; we took that to indicate a measure of acceptance.

Despite my fears we had, so far, managed to avoid any serious mishaps with pleasure boats but, as we moved proudly along the congested stretch between the Brays' boat and the old Willow Wren yard, we encountered the narrow boat cruiser *Ironweed*. The boat's steerer, happily chatting to someone on the towpath, seemed unconcerned, or unaware of our careful progress past the unbroken line of moored craft. It would have been a simple matter to have slipped by, but he suddenly looked up, panicked, and did all the wrong things, ending up broadside across the cut. I eased *Comet* into reverse and revved hard, but could not prevent a

30 Ernie (background) watches until the boats move out of sight and pride, once more . . .

31 (overleaf) . . . comes before a fall. The collison with *Ironweed*

glancing blow which resulted in a mêlée of boats; and a chaotic scene in, as ever, the most public of places. Feeling rather sheepish, I steered the motor into the bottom lock and as the pair ascended, it became apparent that a wooden cant² on *Comet*'s bow was damaged; Ian was not amused.

Dennis Clarke's parents, Hubert and Thirza, ran the 'Admiral Nelson' in the sixties, so we were careful not to nip in for a quick half when we should have been working, but we would often walk up to the pub if we were stopping over at the yard. Leslie Morton held court in the bar on Wednesdays and David Blagrove recounts such an audience, and in so doing describes the interior as I remember it, in his book *Bread Upon the Waters*:

The bar of the 'Nelson' was empty save for Leslie Morton; a wizened ancient wearing a trilby and scarf and the landlord – a fat, balding, middle-aged man who glared at us grumpily. Our opening the door set an electric bell ringing and the landlord said brusquely, 'Boock oop and shoot that bloody door!'

Morton bought us a pint each, placing his change in a pile on the bar, and I looked round to take stock. There were two rooms knocked into one, the bar occupying the smaller part. The larger room had a door at the far end leading into a games room and the door by which we had entered on the canal side. On a wall adjoining the games room was the dartboard and, opposite the entrance door, stood an upright piano. Another door led out to the Gents and Ladies. Along the canalside wall ran a cushioned bench and there were several iron-framed tables and stools. These continued into the smaller part, down one side of which ran the bar. Behind it were the usual stock shelves which also contained chocolate, sweets, nuts, Ringer's A1 Light, Old Holborn, Rizla cigarette papers, Woodbine and Park Drive packets. Beside the hand pulls for beer stood a wooden firkin from which the landlord would occasionally draw himself a half pint. A clock ticked on the wall at the end of the bar above an iron grate. The landlord had the racing page of the 'Daily Mirror' before him and was trying to persuade the others to back a horse that had taken his fancy.[3]

Now, I entered the 'Nelson' at one end of a smart, carpeted room; the bar, with a delightful collection of lace plates above it ran, as before, along the left hand side. Benches, now sporting the obligatory chintzy cushions, still occupied the canalside wall, under windows which framed a timeless, unchanging view of the lock and the hillside beyond, dotted with grazing sheep.

Assorted bottles and jars stood on shelves by the York stone fireplace, with pride of place given to what must surely be the only football trophy in England painted in traditional canal style – a sort of cross between a Buckby can and the FA Cup! The legend, 'Braunston Five-a-side Runners Up', stood out among the painted roses and in the band around the middle normally reserved for the name of a boat, 'Admiral Nelson' was painted in shaded lettering. On the wall above the piano was a cabinet containing more conventional sporting trophies and there was a gallery of photographs of the competing teams. Signed portraits of succeeding Mikron Theatre groups, who regularly perform their canal entertainments in the pub, jostled with the footballers and darts players, and a framed certificate proclaimed the hostelry '3rd in the Pub of the Year Competition'.

At the far end, the games room with its skittle alley was much as it used to be, but looked more austere in comparison with its luxurious neighbour. There were no old boaters to be seen but, sitting behind half a pint of ale at the next table, was a young man wearing wire-framed spectacles and a wispy beard. He was talking obsessively, in a voice calculated to be overheard, about 'Rickys' and 'Peters Two' and how brilliantly he had boated from 'Blis'orth' to 'Maffers', and he was bending the ear of another boring young man in wire-framed glasses and beard. Outside, the pair exchanged 'in' jokes with fellow enthusiasts passing through the lock aboard narrow boats that had every rope, can and brass in exactly the right place, at exactly the right angle. Joyce Fox once said to me that watching Arthur and Ernie working through a lock was like watching a ballet; a bit fanciful, perhaps, but watching

32 Looking from the towpath footbridge towards the Willow Wren yard, mid-60s . . .

33 . . . and 1985, with *Comet* and *Barnes* approaching the bottom lock

34&35 Two shots of the Pub Lock, one in carrying days and the other during the leisure boom. No prizes for guessing which picture is from which period!

these people shouting instructions and rushing up and down was, without doubt, a pantomime!

We squeezed successfully by a steady procession of boats in Braunston tunnel until some Jack-the-Lads on a hire boat found themselves on a collision course with *Barnes*. One, kneeling precariously on the bow, automatically thrust out a hand to fend off the butty and only a frantic shout from Harry, standing in the hold just behind the cratch, prompted him to withdraw it before it was crushed. We reached the infamous dog-leg (created when the teams boring from either end had to change course slightly in order that they should meet in the middle) at precisely the same moment as the 70ft camping boat *Crane*. It has been known for full length boats to get wedged at this point and I blanched at the thought, but we scraped through.

Brigadier Fielding, standing in the garden of the little toll house at Norton Junction, waved a greeting as we passed and the sight of the loaded boats must have stirred many memories for this Salvationist who worked with the boat people until 1964, travelling the canals aboard narrow boats *Aster* and *Salvo*.[4]

My own memory was jogged by the sight of the Leicester Section of the Grand Union winding away towards the Soar and the Trent. We took timber this way and met problems seldom encountered by steerers more used to working in comparative safety on narrow and still watered canals. The Trent, which carried sea-going vessels, was wide and swift flowing and at each lock entrance an unprotected weir threatened the unwary. The best way to avoid trouble was to go like stink past each torrent, throw the motor into reverse and stop, hopefully, before you hit the lock gates.

On one particular evening, pushing on hard to reach the next lock and a safe mooring before dark, we passed a sign carrying the warning: KEEP LEFT SUBMERGED WALL in large red letters. I was wondering how far left I should steer when *Comet* reared up and stopped dead in the middle of the navigation. I prodded around frantically with the long shaft but could not reach the bottom, which would have offered some leverage to work the boat clear. I was concerned that the motor's wooden bottom may have been damaged, and all the time the gloom was gathering. Night boating was part and parcel of carrying on the cut, but in these unfamiliar and hostile waters it was positively dangerous.

Luckily, we had been spotted by the local Sea Scouts, who interrupted their boat-handling class and came to our aid in a dinghy. The rescue party returned to the shore with lines and about fifty excited boys eventually heaved the boats clear. With no suitable mooring at hand, we had no alternative but to continue our journey in total darkness, the probing beam of the headlamp unable to reach either bank of the river.

We moved gingerly ahead with eyes and ears straining and then, almost inaudible at first above the noise of *Comet*'s engine, I heard the sinister murmuring of a weir. As we drew closer, the din grew louder and louder in the blackness until, confused and frightened, I could not tell where the fearful roar was coming from. Then I saw a light and in desperation, pointed the bow straight for it in the faint hope that it shone from the lock keeper's house. My gamble paid off and, like a beacon, it guided us past the weir and on into the sanctuary of the lock.

7

Life Afloat

Our series of incidents with inexperienced, or incompetent, pleasure boaters continued unabated. As we descended the top lock at Long Bucky another hire boat, this time steered by a youth mentally locked behind the wheel of his customised Escort, came steaming round the blind bend under the road bridge and hit the bottom gates with an almighty thump. The gates shuddered under the impact and the hire boat lurched backwards down the cut as if reeling from a fatal blow. Had it happened a few seconds later, with the gates opening, or our motor's bow thrusting out of the lock, I hate to think what the consequences might have been. As we passed, I remonstrated with the offender, but he seemed rather perplexed by all the fuss.

At Long Buckby, the canal is joined by the main London–Midland railway line and the M1 motorway, and for a short distance three ages of transport share the same route. The swifter railways had overtaken canals in the middle of the nineteenth century, only to be left behind in turn by the door-to-door convenience of road haulage in the twentieth. In the 1960s, canals were clinging to a tiny proportion of the trade and I, I suppose, ought to have been speeding down the motorway behind the wheel of a heavy lorry, instead of steering a narrow boat at little more than walking pace on the cut.

It was getting dark as we made our way through Blisworth and approached the tunnel, which had been reopened eleven months before after a four year closure. Dangerous bulges in the brick lining and floor prompted a comprehensive survey to be undertaken in 1980 and this showed that the problems were most acute in the middle third of the tunnel. Concealed construction shafts and water inflows had ducted water down to the old brickwork and pressure had built up on the wet brick from surrounding clay, which expanded when waterlogged.

A bold and radical solution was proposed: to replace the entire brick lining with a pre-cast concrete lining in the middle section of the tunnel, a length of some 1,000 metres. A specially constructed machine was built into a cylindrical steel shield, assembled inside the tunnel. The shield moved along the tunnel as work progressed, acting as protection to both men and machinery. Brickwork at the north and south ends had not deteriorated as badly, and so could be retained after being repaired and repointed.

This operation was actually more difficult than building a new tunnel. It began in August 1982 with the damming of the northern two-thirds of the tunnel to empty it of water, and the laying of a concrete road on the tunnel floor to enable vehicles to reach the central area where the major construction work would take place.

The impressive 'brick-eating' machine consisted basically of an hydraulic excavator mounted within the steel shield, with a cutting edge at the front. A conveyor system moved the old brick and soil back behind the machinery for loading on to articulated dump trucks. These reversed down the tunnel to unload concrete segments, and drove forwards out of the tunnel when re-loaded with excavated bricks and waste.

The pre-cast concrete lining segments, unloaded in the tunnel, were laid flat and fed through to the construction area on the conveyor. There was no space to change their order, and neither were they always identical, so it was vital to load and unload them in order of assembly. The shield formed a 'working chamber' inside which . . . (the) workforce could put the new, segmented concrete rings in place, using sophisticated, laser-controlled alignment techniques. As each ring was completed, the steel shield and its mechanical contents moved forward to prepare for the next – not only protecting the work-force, but also supporting the tunnel until the new lining was in place. For some metres ahead of the shield, steel arches were erected to support the old brickwork – and then moved down the tunnel as the shield progressed. So smooth did the whole operation become that eventually one entire 750 mm-wide segmented concrete ring was erected every hour, an advance of some 15 metres each day.

Hillmorton Locks

6   Breasted-up for the Marsworth flight

Hanwell Locks

8   *Comet* and *Barnes* at Gayton Junction, February 1965

Throughout the work, the team took care to provide for re-connection of the old ventilation shafts and drainage systems, and proceeded cautiously where the old construction shafts met the tunnel lining and had become blocked with clay. The gap behind the new concrete lining was filled with cement grout.

One practical feature of the new section that less-than-expert boatmen will appreciate is the incorporation of a timber-faced fender in the casting at each side of the tunnel – designed to prevent damage to boats and the new lining.

At the end of the re-lining work, completed in 1983, well ahead of schedule, the machinery was dismantled and taken out of the tunnel, but the steel shield could not be removed. After this came the final touches – repairing and re-connecting ventilation shafts and the drainage system, renovating the imposing brick portals at each end of the tunnel, and removing the concrete road and dams. All that remained was for the historic tunnel to be flooded and re-opened to traffic on 22nd August 1984, by Sir Leslie Young CBE, DL, Chairman of British Waterways Board, a whole six months earlier than had been expected.[1]

Barnes' improvised headlamp, run off, and propped against, a car battery on the cabin roof, attracted thousands of darting, dancing greenfly; but in the depths of the tunnel, they were drowned by a deluge of falling water and the cabin top was littered with bodies and a handful of pathetic, stumbling survivors.

We thundered through the very impressive new section like a train in the London underground and as we neared the far end of the tunnel, two pairs of luminous eyes flashed in the beam of the headlamp. Emerging into the more hospitable darkness of a starry night, we were challenged by two barking Alsatians and tied up at the end of a long and eventful, though not altogether unsatis-factory, day.

We were up at six and making ready to leave, when a big Dutch barge crept by, heading north. The vessel was setting off early in order to inconvenience as few people as possible, for she would need all of the tunnel to herself. We had noticed a sign on the northern portal the previous evening warning of her intended passage. She was an incongruous sight on the canal, her great bulk dwarfing *Comet* and *Barnes*, our indigenous craft. Her steerer wore a flowing red beard and stood in a wheel-house at the stern. On the deck, beneath the lowered mast, were oil drums and lengths of timber, three bikes and a flower garden in terracotta pots.

We set off ourselves after the barge had gone and emerged from the chill and shadowy cutting into an unsullied morning, clean and still, with dew glistening in the grass and the sun rising in a clear blue sky. With *Comet*'s barking engine cutting the silence, we intruded into Stoke Bruerne's Sunday morning slumber and the curtains stirred in an upstairs cottage window.

Apart from noticing one or two additional buildings, the shop adjoining the Waterways Museum and the insensitive restaurant extension to the Boat Inn, I was seeing Stoke much as I remembered it. But the old canal atmosphere is a fragile thing and one has to be up early to savour it these days; for Stoke Bruerne is more usually overrun by children with clip-boards, descending in their hundreds from coaches in the pay-and-display car park and by picnickers and rally-goers and teams of Morris dancers. Sadly, commercialisation rules at this 'pretty' location, but by 'selling' the waterways, making them pay their way, the essence of their original appeal is lost in the rush.

Tony Conder, Curator of the Museum, appeared at the top lock, having driven over the hill from his home at Blisworth to see the boats, and the well known canal writer, boatman and singer David Blagrove waited for us further down, his moped parked at the lock side and his windlass nestling on his shoulder under his jacket, having ridden at speed from his cottage in Stoke Bruerne.

By Yardley Gobion where, just before my own carrying days, David had written of hearing '. . . the hollow punting of a football and the shouts of the players in the distance . . .' I heard the thrashing of a helicopter.[2] Soon afterwards a second flew over, and a third, and puzzling over the procession, I remembered that it was Grand Prix day at Silverstone. A motor racing fan had told me once that the only way for participants and well-heeled spectators to avoid the notoriously congested approach roads to the circuit

36 Intruding into Stoke's Sunday morning slumber. The new
restaurant is on the left, the Museum on the right

was to fly in. At one point, they swept so frequently and noisily over the hill that I was reminded of a sequence from Francis Ford Coppola's *Apocalyse Now*, where American combat helicopters bearing the legend 'Death from Above', fly in battle formation to destroy a Vietnamese village with their loudspeakers blaring out Wagner's 'Ride of the Valkyries'.

Then came Milton Keynes, the biggest and most obvious alteration to the old canal landscape, a city where, previously, there had been villages and open fields. In 1962, Buckinghamshire County Council, anxious to prevent London from swallowing up large areas of south Bucks and the Chilterns, earmarked a site in the north of the county to accommodate the overspill. Encompassing the three towns of Stony Stratford, Wolverton and Bletchley, and thirteen villages, the site became the largest, totally planned new urban development in British town planning history. According to chairman Sir Henry Chilver, Milton Keynes Development Corporation, in close co-operation with the British Waterways Board, have '. . . striven to make the Grand Union Canal a special feature . . .' of the city.[3] So what have their efforts achieved along the thirteen miles of canal, from Cosgrove in the north to Stoke Hammond in the south, that come within the city boundary? Well, not much! The results may best be described as bland.

It was all pleasant enough, with grassy banks and gravel paths, benches and picnic tables and the cut itself, though full of weed, was remarkably free of rubbish for an urban waterway. The city's industrial sites do not impose on the canal, but housing developments abound. 'Pennylands', perhaps the boldest example, is built around three arms connected to the Grand Union and has forty units comprising luxury houses and bungalows, and flats which display a strong Japanese influence. Most have bottom of the garden moorings.

Due, perhaps, to financial restraints, the differences between one development and the next are superficial, changes of colour and materials (red or yellow bricks, red or grey tiles) and varying styles cannot camouflage a distinct and depressing conformity, symbolised by the mandatory chocolate brown window frames. It was very neat and orderly, almost twee, and if those walking along

37 Waterways paying their way. '. . . picnickers and rally-goers and teams of Morris dancers', seen from the upper floor of the Museum

the towpath were representative, populated entirely by young marrieds with small children. Milton Dreams springs to mind as a more apt name for the place.

How different the life-style and expectations of these young people in Milton Keynes, and their counterparts in the sixties, from those Pat and I shared with the youngsters on the working boats. The boat people moved about their linear kingdom shrinking from an alien and forbidding world on the other side of the towpath hedge, a world for which canals were nothing more than convenient tips for discarded washing machines and old bicycles. Many, even in 1964, were illiterate, and though some possessed a wireless, and portable televisions were not unknown, they showed little interest in events 'on the bank'. Their conversation was limited by this naivety and concerned their own insular world; they talked about where they had been and where they were going, about the state of the cut and the frequency of trips.

But many of their teenage sons and daughters, though still wary of the outside world, were less intimidated and harboured a vague and brooding notion that there was something more to life, something better on the other side. The seed of their restlessness sown, perhaps, during stays at the boat children's school in Birmingham, grew stronger under the influence of the handful of young people like us who had joined the boats from 'off the land'.

The life we shared, in a world almost unchanged since the 'canal mania' of the 1790s, differed dramatically from those of our teenage contemporaries for, in the summer of 1964, England was gripped by another kind of fever. It was called 'Beatlemania'. While, in the public bar of the New Inn or the Admiral Nelson, the Greyhound or the Six Bells at Brentford, we enjoyed a singsong, or some old boy step-dancing to scratchy 78s played on a wind-up gramophone, The Beatles music and image had taken the country by storm, provoking saturation coverage in the media. Their records sold by the million and 100,000 kids turned up to catch a glimpse of their idols at Liverpool Town Hall. In London, shops and market stalls were decked with bunting and every saleable item seemed to carry their picture.

At the Boatmen's Mission in Brentford, the boaters paid Mr

Chapman a few pennies for someone's old overcoat or demob suit, while in the carnival atmosphere of Carnably Street, office boys and shop girls spent their wages in boutiques, on the flamboyant new clothes of John Stephen and Mary Quant. These fashions, along with motor scooters, rhythm 'n' blues and pep pills, were the identifying symbols of the Mod, while the Rockers, greasy throw-backs to the Teddy Boys of the fifties, rejected the new styles and clung to their leather jackets and powerful bikes, rock 'n' roll and transport caffs. Almost every weekend, on the beaches at Margate, Hastings, or Clacton, they did battle, while the teenage boaters, remote from all the mayhem, simply hankered for a steady factory job and a secondhand Ford Consul. They still courted each other along the cut, as their parents and grandparents had done, and under the A5 road bridge at Fenny Stratford, 'Leslie Ward loves Janit Harris' was still scrawled on the wall.

It was a miserable, drizzling morning in Leighton Buzzard and we needed provisions so, having decided to forfeit an early start and wait for the shops to open in the town, we set about emptying chemical toilets, replenishing our supply of water and generally attending to things domestic. *Barnes* now had the luxury of a large water tank in the fore-end and a sink in her small cabin extension, but in the old days our store was carried in five Buckby cans on the cabin roofs. There was an adequate network of taps along the cut and we used their contents, in preference to the murky brown stuff from the canal, to keep ourselves (relatively) clean.

Clothes presented more of a problem. Small items could be accommodated in the dipper, a traditionally painted bowl with a handle, but our jeans were lashed to the butty's rudder and washed in the cut while the boats were underway. When an opportunity presented itself, while waiting for orders, or during a delay in loading or unloading, the less hard wearing garments were taken to the nearest launderette and we visited the local public baths for a long-awaited and self indulgent soak.

The most trying of the domestic chores in the sixties was the constant struggle to keep the cabins clean from the effects of the solid fuel stove and the fine coal dust that settled on everything

38 (above) Teenage
boaters and
39 (right) Mods
outnumbering
two fleeing
Rockers whose
only escape is to
jump off the roof
of Brighton
Aquarium

during loading and unloading. The interior surfaces, which were not scumbled in the traditional manner, but retained their standard British Waterways cream paint, had continually to be washed down.

Not all the boat people took as much trouble over their personal hygiene, or the cleanliness of their craft. You could smell some of them a mile away and many of the boat cabins were infested with bugs. When the boats were docked at Braunston, the cabins were sealed with wet sacks and fumigated.

Dennis Clarke: We put two bloody great sulpher candles in one little cabin; it wouldn't be the first time that a cabin was set on fire and you bailed out a bit quick when you lit them buggers. But you didn't win then. All the cabins were built with tongue and groove boards and the bugs got in there. When the first insecticide sprays came out we thought it was the end of the world!

But I've known boats where you could have eaten your dinner off the floor of the hold, let alone the cabin; they used to get down on their hands and knees and scrub the boats out, clean as a new pin.

We finally loosed our moorings at half past ten, but travelled only a few yards before *Comet* went aground. After several minutes manoeuvring she was freed and as we got underway again, passing through the narrow gap between the abutments of a dismantled swing bridge, I stepped ashore from *Barnes'* fore-end and was handed a bike to do my stint of lock-wheeling. I peddled determinedly off with the rain, driven now by a howling wind, sweeping in waves across the cut, and moved along the derelict brick wharf where the Blue Line boats had loaded sand for Paddington. The narrow gauge railway track was still in place and I remembered the Brays loading here from little tipping trucks.

With the rain lashing my face and soaking my trousers, I gained the high ground at Grove Lock and looked back, only to see *Comet*'s progress halted again a hundred yards short of the lock. 'The Fields', that stretch from Leighton to Marsworth, notorious

40   Rain and a howling wind across 'The Fields'

among the boaters for its shallowness appeared, over twenty odd years, to have kept its reputation intact.

Our income on the working boats was directly related to productivity; the more trips we made, the more money we earned. But many factors, not least the poor state of the cut, contrived to frustrate us. Stretches of canal, particularly the Coventry, were shallow and in poor condition; bends were unprotected by piling and mud was continually pulled into the cut by the wash from passing boats. Matters were made even worse by a firm in Nuneaton pumping in slurry from their gravel workings.

There were no qualms about polluting the canal. Going down through Birmingham was like boating through treacle; the lock walls all dripping and you had to throw away your ropes after bow-hauling. Wooden boats didn't need bitumen, their hulls were coated in the cut, completely oiled.

Antiquated and inefficient methods of loading and unloading were the final straw. Stacking wood by hand was back-breaking work and there was always the chance of getting a splinter like a dagger in your hand. The grabs employed to scoop coal out of the boats never reached the edges, so we stood in the bottom scraping the dust into the centre for the buckets. It was filthy work and we often peered over the gunnels to see a lorry simply open its tail-board and tip its load straight into the required place. On top of all this, we hung around for hours, or even days, waiting for our turn at the wharf. A trip might have taken three or four days, but when the time for loading and unloading was added on, that could easily be stretched to ten.

Not all the boaters shared our concern. Some exacerbated the situation by waiting around to see members of their family who worked on other boats, and some were just apathetic. The situation was bad enough for Willow Wren to circulate the instructions to all their steerers which are reproduced overleaf.

With a 50 ton load, a pair would lose £2 10s 0d (£2.50) a day for every day they were overdue in delivering and that was no small sum when subtracted from the £20 or £25 earned from a trip. But for many of the boat families, no such incentives were necessary. They thought nothing of working a seventeen hour day and it

STANDING ORDERS TO BOATMEN

From our craft control it has been noted that some steerers do not make the best of their way when loaded. In other words, there is too much hanging about. From the time you receive this notice, you are responsible for getting to your destination as quickly as possible. You are reminded that cargoes in your craft are required for immediate use by manufacturers. Undue delay on your part, will eventually mean that freight will be lost to the canal and, in the long run you, the boatmen, will be the ones to suffer.

INSTRUCTIONS TO BE OBEYED.

(1) The hold of all craft shall be clean and tidy at all times. If you receive orders to load wheat you must make protection to keep the floors dry.

(2) Craft discharging in Birmingham, will proceed to Coalfields via Saltley.

(3) Pairs of boats, will load no more than 50/51 tons. Weights above this, which cause delays, will not be paid for.

(4) Travelling times

Baddesley / Croxley	$4\frac{1}{4}$ days
Newdigate / Rickmansworth	$3\frac{1}{2}$ days
Brentford / Birmingham	5 days
Brentford / Wellingborough	4 days
Brentford / Bletchley	$2\frac{1}{4}$ days
Brentford / Tipton	$5\frac{1}{2}$ days

These are the times you will be allowed, if you fail to observe these times your freight rate will be decreased by 1/-d. per ton per day for all days in excess.

(5) Wheat and Corn

Steerers will load no more than approx:- 50 tons, unless instructed specially to load more. The last pair of boats will then get a fair proportion of the shipment.

Date.......5th November, 1964.

would never have occurred to them to do a trip in anything but the fastest possible time. It was a simple matter of self respect, of pride in their ability to go quicker than the others and to earn a decent living.

No amount of effort with the shaft, or thrashing away in forward or reverse, would shift *Comet* off the mud below Grove Lock, so I resorted to flushing water through and, finally, the motor lurched forward, snatching *Barnes* into sudden motion behind. We negotiated the lock, and with heads bent against the arrowing rain, battled on to the next. It was a desolate scene above Church Lock, where the wind whipped the surface of the canal into a choppy sea and worried at a string of boats fidgeting agitatedly at their moorings. Among these was *Redcap*, once owned by Colonel Ritchie, former adjutant of the South Staffordshire Regiment and Provost Marshal of West Berlin.

The Colonel was a Willow Wren director and was ferried around the canals by the boatmen, who considered being batman on such a tour of inspection an easy option compared with working a pair. Colonel Ritchie and his wife lived at Stoke Bruerne and one or other of them would usually turn out when boats were passing. Mrs Ritchie was a small woman with a reputation among the boat people for being rather severe in her moral attitudes so, whenever we approached the village, Pat would turn her engagement ring around in imitation of a wedding band, in case the old lady should give us a sermon on the sanctity of marriage.

The huge cement works at Ivinghoe shrouded, as the surrounding countryside also seemed to be, in white dust, still dominated the landscape as we climbed steadily towards the Tring summit. Halfway up Marsworth Locks, we were halted again by something substantial around the prop. We prodded and jabbed with the boat hooks, feeling around the shaft and blade for a hold, then twisted and tugged and jerked for all we were worth. We gingerly engaged forward and reverse in an effort to unwind whatever was tangled there and, gradually, a fragment at a time, disgorged a pile of debris onto the lock side which included two fishermen's keep nets and yards of cable, presumably discarded when the adjacent telephone wires were repaired.

I swear *Comet* shuddered as we passed the Wendover Arm (where the old boat had been left for dead) and we fairly fled into the Tring cutting; but the summit pound was constructed with a greater depth than was usual so that it could act as a reservoir, and this *may* have accounted for the sudden turn of speed. When I was boating in the sixties, this deep and heavily wooded cutting was showing signs of neglect, but in the mid-seventies British Waterways completed an ambitious scheme to improve the Grand Union between Soulbury and Northchurch, promoting it as a showpiece in the hope that Government would release funds for similar work elsewhere. Now, alas, the cutting had been allowed to deteriorate once more, with overgrown trees drastically reducing the usable width of the canal, and I wondered if all the effort and money expended on the scheme had been worthwhile.

Tied above Cowroast Lock, as if waiting for clearance to descend to the paper mills, but actually holidaying aboard their wooden cabin cruiser, were ex-Willow Wren captain Ron Withy and family. The Cowroast had been a traffic control point where boats were held up to prevent congestion further down at Dickinson's mills at Apsley and Croxley Green.

As we approached the wide lock, Ian slowed the motor, and as the butty crept closer, coiled in the towing line and dropped it neatly onto *Barnes'* bow. Some gentle rowing with the tiller sent the butty gliding into the lock beside the now stationary motor and the lock-wheeler wound a stout rope from her bow around a bollard to check her advance. I slid the heavy curved tiller out of its slot in the ram's head and laid it on the cabin top and as I stepped onto the lock side, the bottom paddles were raised. Then, following an initial push the top gates, helped by the surge of water out of the lock, banged shut behind the boats.

As *Comet* and *Barnes* began to descend, we each took a line, I from the mast of the butty, Ian from the motor, passed it between the hand rails on the bottom gates and tied it in a slip knot against one of the uprights. I slipped the eye of another line over the small stud on the lock side by the top gate and stepped down into *Barnes'* cockpit. When the lock was empty, the motor went astern, pulling its gate open with the line from the hand-rail. The butty moved back of its own accord, opening its gate in turn, and as the rudder clattered against the sill at the back of the lock, I took a turn with my stern line around the 'T' stud on the back deck. As the motor moves forward, the butty tries to follow it out and the line, drawn suddenly taught and creaking under the strain, checks the forward thrust.

As *Comet* moved out of the lock, the gate-opening line undid itself and fell into the hold, and as her counter passed *Barnes'* bow, Ian reached across and took the towing line, slipping the eye over one of the stern studs. As he did so I loosed the line from the butty's stern and, with a deft flick of the wrist, sent a curve racing up the line and the eye jumped off the lock side stud. The motor tugged at the dipping tow rope and *Barnes'* bow lurched crazily sideways (on collision course with the lock wall), before straightening suddenly and leaping forward in pursuit.

We were passing out of the lock, content with an accomplished performance, when Ron Withy was heard to say, 'Not bad Harry, but you're loaded wrong!'

Buttying down to Berkhamsted in the late afternoon was a joy, for the turbulent weather at last gave way to a still evening and a pale sun and we fell easily, now, into a routine at each lock. We passed through the town at dusk, tying up in pitch darkness and seclusion at Bourne End, and in *Barnes'* primitive galley, cooked mince, potatoes and peas in one saucepan, ate it all greedily and mopped our plates with wedges of bread.

41   (overleaf) The line from the lock-side stud checking the forward thrust of the butty

8

Past All The Old Places . . . To Brentford

We tumbled out at five to find a beautiful morning, heavy with mist and dew; a child would, instinctively, have written something with his finger in the dewy film glistening on the cabin sides. The sun peeped through the squat trees lining the canal, glinting on the brass chimney bands and, in the distance, the white handrails and white-tipped beams of a lock could just be made out through the dripping, grey-gold after-dawn.

But the clatter of *Comet*'s engine and the rattle of paddle gear pierced the damp silence as I set off, once more, on the bike. By the 'Three Horseshoes' at Winkwell, I opened the iron swing bridge by means of the huge revolving wheel and, as one or two cars waited impatiently in the lane, closed it again behind the boats. I hurried on by the watercress beds to lock 62, where the railway runs parallel to the canal on an embankment, shielding the busy A41 on the other side; but resting on the balance beam while the lock filled, I enjoyed perfect solitude, with only darting, swooping house-martins for company. Then, I heard the persistent beat of the PD2 under the railway bridge and *Comet*'s bow nosed round the bend, cutting the glass-like water.

At Fishery Lock, the birds gave way to a procession of sober-suited men with brief cases, who frowned continually at their wrist watches as they hurried across the bridge to Hemel Hempstead station and the 7.35 to Euston. Under the bridge, among the inevitable 'Mods Rule OK' grafitti, a kindred spirit had daubed 'Bring Back Narrow Boat Carrying Soon'.

A bald, middle-aged man in a track suit jogged around the

cricket field by Boxmoor Lock as I waited for the boats. He had managed six painful looking circuits on the sodden grass before *Comet* limped into the lock, slowed by what turned out to be the remains of the telephone wire picked up at Marsworth, which had been trailing in the water and hooking more debris as we went along.

I made a detour at the next bridge; there had been a little general stores, favoured by the boaters, about a hundred yards from the canal, and as we needed milk and tea, I peddled off in search of it, wondering if it had been forced out of business, like so many others, by the supermarket chains. But it was still there, run by a Pakistani family, with a small boy busily making up sandwich orders for the mill and factory workers. The 'corner shop' would surely not have survived without them.

The damp and chill of the early morning was wilting under a strengthening sun as we dropped down past Dickinson's Apsley and Nash paper mills. Both still used coal, but we passed the large stocks by the canal lamenting the fact that it had all been delivered by road. We passed the Barratts and the Boswells, heading north at a rate of knots, on the return leg of a holiday cruise to Paddington. They steered the wooden river cruisers favoured by many ex-boaters, presumably for their turn of speed.

Gazing absently across the fields as we approached Lady Capel's Lock, my attention was suddenly focused on a tiny figure breaking cover from a distant wood and running downhill towards the canal. I half expected to see a pack of dogs, or policemen, in pursuit, but instead, another figure followed. As they drew closer, I saw that they were wearing jerseys and shorts and that others were filing down the track behind. By the time the boats were descending in the lock, the leaders were puffing, heavy legged, along the towpath, their faces crimson with the effort and the heat. Then I recognised a dusky fellow with jutting knees and it dawned on me that they were Watford footballers undergoing the torture of pre-season training. Poor John Barnes was a long, long way from the glory of his goal against Brazil in the Maracana![1]

We glided majestically through the handsome Georgian bridge (164), then spoiled the effect by having to pull out all the stops negotiating the particularly sharp bend before Cassiobury Locks. The beauty of 'The Parks' was misleading, for *Comet* got stuck on the sill coming out of Watford Lock and again under bridge 168 where Ian, prodding a shaft down to test the depth, retrieved it with a bicycle wheel hanging on the end and shouted, 'It's solid down there!'

Dickinson's huge mill at Croxley Green had dominated the canal landscape. A succession of open-fronted sheds, containing bales of paper, ran along the cut before a mass of large buildings and beyond, almost at the mouth of Common Moor Lock, stood the unloading gear. An endless bucket chain was dropped down to the hold and while this went inexorably round and round, we would stand on either side, shovelling coal into the buckets.

Now, amazingly, not a trace remained. The buildings, the sheds and the mechanical equipment had all disappeared and all one saw from the canal was a grassy bank, sparsely planted with saplings, presumably intended to screen the cut from the view of the workers who will be employed in the massive new complex under construction on the other side. Is the canal considered an eyesore, or a distraction, by the captains of industry? Or were they compelled to hide their modern 'satanic mills' from the pleasure boaters' gaze?

In July 1964, Pat and I were nearing the end of our first trip, for now there were only a couple of miles to go before we reached the sewage works at Maple Cross. First, however, we had to attend to some business at Stockers Lock, where the Waterways lock keeper was also employed by Willow Wren to distribute monies to their boatmen. I collected £23 10s 0d (£23.50) in cash and a slip of paper detailing payments and deductions (see Appendix IV).

We had earned 14s. (70p) per ton for the 49 tons 11 cwt carried, plus an extra 10s. (50p) for helping to empty the boats (a task we had still to perform on arrival at the works), a total of £35 3s 8d (£35.20). After deducting national insurance contributions and income tax, Willow Wren made a nominal charge of £1 for the hire of the boats and banked £5 for reserve credit. This last payment was deducted after each trip so that the boatmen would accumulate a sum to pay for any breakdowns or repairs which might

42   Willow Wrens waiting to unload at Croxley Mill. The unloading equipment can be seen on page 135

43   Nothing left of Croxley Mill in 1985

44   But the Sewage Works was still there. The smell, at least, had not changed

occur. Additionally, Pat and I paid £1 3s 0d (£1.15) towards the purchase price of the Calor Gas cooker left by Jack Hatchard.

Willow Wren issued their *Standing Orders to Boatmen* in the November following our first trip and under the criteria contained in that document, our 1985 effort may have escaped incurring penalty charges. The time allowed for the trip from Newdigate to Rickmansworth was three and a half days. We set off at 6pm on Friday, making three days to 6pm Monday. Having reached Stockers at 2pm on Tuesday (and the Sewage Works a little after) we may just have avoided the 1s (5p) per ton penalty imposed for exceeding the stated time. The actual boating time was 54 hours from Sutton Stop to the Sewage Works. I had suffered nagging doubts that we would complete the trip at all, and to have achieved a time roughly comparable with that demanded in the sixties, was beyond my expectations (See Appendix V).

Stockers Lock had changed not at all. The white lock cottage with the tall chimneys still looked like a single storey building until a glance over the low wall running along its front reminded one that the door and windows facing the lock are, in fact, on the first floor and the ground floor sits below in a pretty garden, level with the bottom of the lock. The row of curved bricks along the top of the wall were freshly painted in white, as were the hand-rails on the gates and the tips of the beams, and the gate leading to the cottage door. Among the flower beds in front, there was a life-belt in a wooden housing and tubs containing more flowers, and on the opposite side of the lock, rose bushes and clipped grass. Over-looking this vision, a fine, ivy-clad, classical house stood by a brick arched bridge and beyond, a majestic field rolled down to the canal and a group of mellow, sixteenth century farm buildings. A perfect spot.

I was lock-wheeling again, leaving Springwell Lock in my wake, as a familiar, pungent whiff gave forewarning of the Sewage Works (not much progress there in twenty one years) and I was soon halted by the steep incline of the iron bridge which carries the towpath over the entrance to the basin where the boats unloaded. Two breasted pairs would reverse under the bridge, the first pair taking up position below a framework of steel girders. An overhead grab swallowed up the coal and regurgitated it into a hopper while we stood, once more, in the hold, earning every penny of our ten bob, scraping crumbs of dust into its greedy jaws.

As at Croxley, the grab and the building it fed had gone (although the sewage works were still operating) and the basin, which provides moorings for an assortment of narrow boats, was separated from the site by a high, wire mesh fence. I would have been very happy on one occasion in the sixties if such a fence had been in place. Many of the boat people had dogs, as pets and to discourage intruders, and Pat and I decided that we needed one too; so, while the boats waited to be unloaded at West Bromwich, we went on the bus into Birmingham and bought a puppy in the market. We called it Hemel.

Back at the wharf, I tied him safely to a Buckby can on the cabin roof and we began unloading the boats. For an hour or two we were engrossed in our work, forgetting all about the animal until Pat looked over to the cabin top. 'Where's the dog?', she said. 'On the cabin roof, tied to the water can', said I; but both had disappeared. I prodded around in the cut with the shaft and with some difficulty, brought out the can. Then, feeling the boat hook catch on something softer, I began to pull again. As the little dog broke the surface of the water, I quickly shook it free, letting it slip back to the bottom of the cut. The boat must have listed, unnoticed, during unloading, tipping puppy and can into the water. The can would quickly have filled up and sunk, anchoring the helpless animal to the bottom. We were very upset by our negligence, but how could we atone for losing the dog?

During a subsequent trip to the sewage works, we decided to buy a more fully grown animal from the Battersea Dogs' Home, convinced that we would be saving some poor stray from certain death. I set off on the underground and arrived at Baker Street clutching my A–Z. I walked along Oxford Street gaping at the shoppers, the roadway teaming with red buses and hustling cabs; past the posh hotels in Park Lane to Belgravia, with its foreign embassies and pied-a-terres; crossed the Thames on Chelsea Bridge, peering down into the heaving brown waters, and watched the tankers and the tugs, with their trains of lighters, ploughing busily up and down. At last, in dismal surroundings, I found myself at the door of the Home.

I chose a mongrel called Nipper, bought a collar and lead with the money I had saved for my bus fare back to Baker Street, and began walking again. It was a long and wearying journey, with the dog constantly tugging at the unnaccustomed leash, so as soon as we arrived at the sewage works, I set him free. Living up to his name, Nipper immediately ran off and to our horror, jumped straight into a settling tank. Somewhat reluctantly, I fished him out with the shaft and threw him into the cut, from which he emerged a little cleaner, and none the worse for his adventure.

On our first trip, the lock keeper at Stockers had advised us that, after unloading, we were to continue south to Willow Wren's depot at Bulls Bridge where we would receive orders for a backload. Although I never saw him there, Leslie Morton ran the company from a prefabricated building at the old British Waterways lay-by. There were plenty of boats in the basin when we arrived. Some crews, like us, were awaiting instructions to proceed to Brentford, where we would meet the lighters which brought aluminium and timber up the Thames from the docks, while others, on their way north, called at the counter in the prefab over which the company conducted its business with the boaters, to collect their starting money (an advance on the amount due at the end of the trip).

Now, the Bulls Bridge Industrial Estate occupied the land behind the lay-by and a complex of factory units ran from one end, where BWB still operate a maintenance yard, to the other. On land, the estate is approached from Hayes Road and leaning against a wall on the corner, an old painted sign lettered 'Willow Wren Wharf' directed callers to an oily boat repair yard where small boats, old engines and spare parts were piled high and guarded by a fierce dog.

The lay-by was packed with boats of all descriptions, but the predominant craft, if they can be described as craft, were the houseboats. Under a forest of television masts, were luxury caravans dropped onto pontoons and purpose-built, two-storey models with neo-Georgian doors and carriage lamps. As we passed, bikini-clad residents on their balconies sipped drinks under 'Martini' umbrellas, unperturbed by the accumulated rubbish in the canal below, or the shabby industrialisation surrounding them.

The recreation ground at Southall was full of Asian families playing cricket, the lowering sun stretching their shadows across the grass and their distant shouts and laughter drifting to the canal on the still evening air. We slowed down by the 'Old Oak Tree' and tied up through the bridge hole by a small green. Three turbaned Sikhs were in animated conversation on a bench and a woman called to her dog in Urdu. I cleaned up quickly and hurried off on the bike in search of some fast food. It was nine o'clock, but the streets were bustling with people and many of the shops, full of sarees, dazzlingly coloured trinkets and exotic food stuffs, were still open for business in King Street and The Green. I caused some amusement in the takeaway as I tried to appear knowledgable over the menu but, in the end, carried a selection of steaming cartons back to the boats in triumph. We sat on the cabin tops in the gathering dusk, tucking into our curry and reminiscing with a middle-aged Indian who remembered the last trading boats on the canal.

We left Southall in no great hurry at half past nine, knowing that it was only a short haul now down to Brentford. The day was already warm and the glare from the white house at Norwood top lock made you screw up your eyes. Sid Cullen, lock keeper at the Hanwell flight since 1961, shuffled out of the adjoining office. He had been a powerful man in the old days, but high blood pressure and arthritis had taken their toll on his large frame and he was looking forward to retirement. He wore a blue Waterways uniform and the sort of peaked cap that railwaymen used to wear; under the cap, his hair was white and his face deeply lined and weather beaten. At a sloping Dickensian desk in the little office, Sid has recorded each boat movement through the lock and the walls were lined with many a dusty volume.

Further down the locks, a BBC crew were making a film for children's television. The cameramen, the girls with the clip-

45   Descending the Hanwell flight

122

boards, and the precocious little girls in the cast were all unconcerned by the passage of the boats, but the director, who
seemed to have little understanding of the significance of a
loaded pair on the canals he was portraying, was most put out
by the interruption. Ex-boatman Ken Dakin, who had been
assigned by the Board to nurse-maid the crew, leaned against the
asylum wall in the sunshine, highly amused by the whole
proceedings.

The flight of six deep locks at Hanwell are accompanied in their
curving descent by a wide gravel towpath and the high perimeter
wall of St. Bernard's Hospital. We dropped down swiftly, pur-
sued by a party of schoolchildren, chattering like monkeys as they
filled in their project sheets, and set off through a variety of
bridges. The first, more like a wide concrete tunnel, carries the
M4 over the canal; then a lofty metal structure accommodates the
Piccadilly Line; the third, built at the Horseley Iron Works in
1820, carries the humble towpath on an elegant cast-iron arch,
every bit as fine as those at Hawkesbury, or Braunston, and all the
more welcome in the south for its rarity.

We left Gallows Bridge behind and, to our surprise, went
aground one last time before the towpath disappeared under the
cathedral-like canopied warehouse at Brent Meadow Wharf. The
boats moved easily into the widening basin and with great relief,
and a little subdued euphoria, came the realisation that we had
actually made it all the way to Brentford.

We tied up on the towpath side, opposite the British Waterways
Freight Services depot where, despite the cranes and forklifts
busying themselves among the warehouses, the lighters alongside
lay idle. A strike in November 1984 finally broke the confidence of
the few companies still carrying by lighter, so the canal is empty of
traffic and the depot is served only by adding to the congestion in
Brentford High Street.

It would not have been unusual in the sixties to see seven or
eight pairs tied up here awaiting the arrival of the lighters which
brought a variety of goods up from the docks. Aluminium, destined for Tyseley Wharf in Birmingham; tomato puree for HP
Beans, to Sampson Road in the same city; wheat for Welling-

46 Tied up at Brentford, opposite the BWB depot

47 Alive with lighters and narrow boats during carrying days. *Comet* and *Barnes* unloaded on the far bank in 1985

borough on the Nene; and redwood and Douglas fir for West Bromwich and Nottingham (see Appendix VI).

Our first back-load had been aluminium ingots which were loaded, as were the wheat and tomato puree, from the warehouse side. Stacked on pallets and lowered into the holds by crane, they should have remained in neat units throughout the journey so they could be unloaded in the same manner in Birmingham, but despite our efforts to steer a steady course, one or two inevitably toppled over, creating a domino effect which left ingots strewn haphazardly about the holds and we were left with the back breaking task of unloading the lot by hand. Timber was loaded from the lighters on the towpath side, but in order to get enough tonnage into the boats, it had to be handled painstakingly by the boaters. The planks, which came in varying lengths, were first laid like a ballroom floor in the bottom of the hold and then, layer upon layer, a huge three-dimensional jig-saw was built up until the required weight was aboard.

Thick with craft, resounding with urgent shouts and the jolting of cranes, Brentford was alive. Now alas, on the water, nothing stirs.

With *Barnham* and *Angel* not due until evening, there was time to visit one or two old haunts, so I walked down past the double gauging locks and, dodging the traffic, crossed the High Street to join the lunch time drinkers in the Six Bells. This was the odd-man-out among the pubs we regularly used in the sixties; it had always been busy with boaters and bargemen, but it surrendered not an inch to the cut, stubbornly retaining the aggressive swagger of a real London boozer and, in many ways, it had stayed truer to its origins than the others.

Brown painted lincrusta and flock-paper still covered the ceilings and walls of the dingy interior, though the red plastic upholstered chairs, and the tubular ornament with the creeping orange liquid on the bar, were not there before. There was a stage in one corner with an upright piano and a sign assuring 'Singers Welcome', but that, I suspect, depends on the popularity of the singer. A list of regulars participating in a pontoon competition run by the *News of the World* was pinned to the wall and read like a

Who's Who in the Underworld: The Hulk, Jack Dash, Fingers, Irish Tom, Fred the Egg, Big Frank, Twinky and Boiler Bill. And at the pool table, the girls with their tattoos looked even tougher than the lads.

After the brash pubs and plate-glass shop fronts of the High Street, The Butts, just around the corner down a nondescript turning, had a quiet 18th century dignity, interrupted only by the Boatman's Institute standing on one side of the square, looking slightly embarrassed, like a plain girl at a party. The Institute, established by the London City Mission in 1904, provided church, maternity home and school for the boat families.

The Mission's contact with the boaters began in 1895 when, out of curiosity, an elderly missionary visited the community and found himself delivering a baby. Mr Woodhall stayed for six years, preaching and teaching the three Rs; he dealt with domestic problems and tended sick horses; became barber and procurer of food and clothes; and he laid out the dead. When the old man retired, he was replaced by a young and energetic missionary named Bamber and it was he who masterminded the building of the Institute and established the services for the boaters. In 1927, just after the General Strike, the Free School at The Ham, with a qualified, paid teacher was put at the disposal of the boat community and beds were made available at various hospitals for expectant mothers; so the first floor at the Institute was converted into a residence for the missionary.

F. J. Chapman was appointed in October 1945, and for the next twenty six years, he conducted Sunday schools and clubs for the boat children and gospel services and meetings for their parents. The Institute was a thriving concern in the sixties and the boat people relied on Mr Chapman to provide more worldly needs; he wrote their letters and read the replies, and for a shilling (5p), he would provide a complete outfit of clothes. He retired on 21st July 1972, by which time the community he served had disappeared from the face of the cut.

48   The Six Bells, Brentford High Street

9

'Save Us Keep Going Up and Down'

At Gayton Arm end, on a frosty morning in February 1965, *Comet* and *Barnes* took longer than usual to get underway. It wasn't the layer of thin ice covering the cut that caused us to linger in the warmth below, but an urgent discussion. We had enjoyed the intimacy imposed by the confines of the narrow boat cabin a little too eagerly; Pat was pregnant! Reluctantly, we decided that she couldn't continue the arduous life of a boatwoman. Pushing and pulling the heavy tiller with all her strength to manoeuvre the big butty, winding ancient and unyielding paddle gear, and loading and unloading cargoes by hand were not prudent occupations for someone in her condition.

After unloading at Dickinson's, I rang Willow Wren from a call box at Croxley Green and explained that we were returning empty and would be leaving the boats at Braunston. They insisted that we pick up a back-load at Brentford but, unlike the boat families, whose dependence on the company for their homes and livelihood prompted them to show undue deference to the depot employees, we had never allowed them to intimidate us. We had even less reason now and I ignored their instructions.

As the Braunston depot had no vehicular access, Pat arranged for her dad to meet us with his van, where the A5 crosses the canal at Long Buckby. Seven months had passed since that warm July morning at the top lock when we moved our few belongings into *Comet*'s cabin from the hotel boats; now we stowed our gear in the back of the van which set off to wait for the boats at Braunston. There were no boaters around the yard to say goodbye to, so we left as quickly as we could; and as we drove north in the van, the only crumb of comfort that tempered my regret was the feeling of relief that I would not be around at the bedside to watch the narrow boat industry in its death throes.

Even in the midst of Willow Wren's energetic rejuvenation of the industry, there were ominous signs that the revival might be short lived. The company had expanded further by taking over British Waterways' north west fleet and business on the Grand Union was brisk, but it seemed doubtful to me whether they could, finally, reverse the prevailing decline. The British Waterways Board report *The Future of the Waterways*, published in January 1964, had indicated that the best hope for the survival of the system might lie in a multi-user policy, incorporating water storage, recreation, and commercial carrying on the major barge waterways. They saw no future for narrow boat carrying! The Board's policy was reflected in the dilapidated state of the cut, and in their refusal to grant the hard won boat licences on a long term basis, thereby giving the carriers some credibility with potential customers.

In January 1967, when I bought the big Woolwich motor *Chiswick* from Willow Wren and started repairing the engine at Braunston, the atmosphere at the yard was gloomy, for the company had just lost the coal traffic to Croxley. Soon after Pat and I had left the boats, Pooley Hall colliery was worked out and the Croxley order was transferred to Donisthorpe, on the Ashby Canal. The trouble was that Donisthorpe had been cut off when a section of the Ashby was closed because of subsidence; Leslie Morton persuaded the National Coal Board to re-mechanise Ilott Wharf at Measham, on the still navigable section, and arranged for the Donisthorpe coal to be delivered there by tipper trucks, so that Willow Wren held on to the traffic.

The Ashby had not seen commercial traffic for years and the first pair, accompanied by a British Waterways dredger, took three days to navigate the canal. The regular passage of the boats improved the channel, but a few months later, proposals were announced to close a further section which included Ilott Wharf. Morton fought the closure plans but a steel dam was erected across the canal so that the water could be drained and the cut was filled in. He considered the closure a death blow for the firm, for several other traffics had been lost, including the timber shipments from Brentford, and all that remained of the regular loads was the coal to the Colne Valley Sewage Works and grain to Whitworth's mill at Wellingborough.

My family was expanding and out-growing our upstairs room in Chapel, so we bought a house, I sold *Chiswick* to pay for the central heating, and it seemed that, finally, all my links with the cut had been severed; but as one door closes, another inevitably opens. I got a new job with a road haulage firm which, ironically, opened another door to canals. I travelled long distances to lorries which had broken down and, employing sometimes outrageous detours, took every opportunity to seek out the cut. I searched for tell-tale clues, a hump backed bridge or a white tipped lock beam and sometimes, across a field, I would catch a glimpse of a boater's head and shoulders, and a smoking chimney, moving steadily along the top of a hedgerow; or I would see, on a grey, wet afternoon, on a filthy cut which lapped the back-side of some dirty Midlands town, the splash of bright colour on the cabin side of a narrow boat. But the boats were increasingly difficult to find.

The Waterways Board's recommendations, contained in the report *Future of the Waterways*, were finally accepted in a Government White Paper: *British Waterways: Recreation and Amenity* in September '67. The waterways were collected into two distinct groups: The first group were to be maintained primarily for commercial transport and the second, to be known as 'cruise-ways', primarily for pleasure craft. The waterways in group one could accommodate large vessels and were considered to have a viable economic future; those collected in group two were the canals built for cargo carrying narrow boats and it was thought that these could no longer usefully form part of a commercial transport system. So, although the future of the canals was secured, the door was officially closed on narrow boat carrying and opened wide for the leisure industry.

At the end of 1967, Willow Wren's north west fleet was taken over by the manager, Alan Galley, trading under the name of the

Anderton Canal Carrying Co and early in 1968, British Waterways repossessed their three dozen boats from the company. Despite this reversal, Leslie Morton was determined to hang on, but Dennis Clarke thought it time to call a halt and moved to Rugby to build up the hire fleet.

Dennis Clarke: I dropped a bombshell. We were flogging our guts out at Braunston making both ends meet in the middle, while the transport side was draining money from the yard and the hire fleet. There was a suite of offices at Bulls Bridge and lots of people, the job just couldn't stand it; it was running into the ground that fast, Leslie should have stopped it.

There was a share shuffle among the directors and I was offered the job of building up the hire cruiser company. It wasn't until the next day that Leslie got to know what I had been up to, but it was too late. We had an up-and-a-downer, its always the same I suppose, the two closest people . . . We'd fought all down the line to make it survive and then, at the end of the day, we had our differences.

The lease for the buildings at Braunston was sold to Chris Barney and then, suddenly, at the end of September, a few months after the death of Capt Bulkeley-Johnson, Leslie Morton died. With him went the last, heroic commitment to narrow boat carrying on the grand scale.

Dennis Clarke: If it had not been for Leslie Morton, there would be no canals. He was a rogue, he knew all the ruddy dodges. He was fighting the Board hammer and tongs; there were court cases flying around to try to make them do something and he lived in the House of Commons. No one else would have had the guts to do what Leslie Morton did; he was a character, there's no doubt about that.

Morton took with him, also, the respect of the boat people.

Ted Ward: He was the reason I went over from British Waterways to Willow Wren. He never used to sit in the office all day and wait for the work to come in, he'd go all over the country to look for it. You couldn't pull the wool over his eyes; if you went into the office and said, 'I've got sixty tons of timber on them two boats', he knowed for a fact they didn't carry sixty tons; he would look through the office window and tell you how much them boats was carrying. I've knowed him to be at Braunston before Dennis Clarke and them come to work, so he could catch them out. He could be the sort of person who'd give you a real good rapping, but once he knowed he'd got through to you he forgot it and that was the end of it all. There were very few people that didn't like him.

If a person worked, he would work with 'em. One of his boats got broken down at eight o'clock at night at Wolverton; they phoned him at Epsom, and he was there at six the next morning with a part for the engine. When I got married, he never even knowed my wife at all, and he gave her a wedding present, a boat's water can, painted like; we've still got it now. And he gave me my very first gas cooker for a boat's cabin. Mind you, he had the money back off me over the years, the amount of work I used to do; but there again, he still done that. I think he was really some'at.

In April 1969, Willow Wren, operating their last half dozen pairs, lost the Wellingborough grain traffic to the railways who quoted a cheaper rate from the new terminal at Tilbury, and in May, because the process for which it was needed had ceased, the last load of coal was delivered to the Colne Valley Sewage Works. After volunteers had repaired the ancient crane at Croxley, the Ashby Canal Association managed to negotiate the resumption of coal deliveries to Dickinson's, but they had continuous trouble with the unloading equipment and it proved difficult to pay an economic rate in the absence of a back-load.

Early in 1970, after negotiations for new traffics had broken down, it was finally decided to wind up Willow Wren's carrying activities and shortly afterwards, Dickinson's announced their intention to change part of their steam raising plant to oil fuel, with the little coal still required coming by lorry. The last load carried by Willow Wren boats left Gopsall Wharf aboard the Ward's *Redshank* and *Ara* on 26th August 1970 and was delivered to Croxley on 3rd September (see Appendix VII). Ted, from a large boating family, had mixed feelings about finishing:

> You went to Gopsall and never knowed when you were going to get loaded, and when you got to Croxley you might have to wait a week for the crane to be repaired. You had to unload the boats yourself and you weren't earning the money you should have been to take a load along the water. I'd had enough of the Croxley run, so I didn't really feel bad that the lot was ending; but I felt sick knowing that the boats I'd worked and looked after for so many years had come to the end and somebody else would have them and probably use them as camping boats or something. But we were pleased for our daughter Julie's sake, it meant she could go to school.

The Blue Line Boats carried their last loads to Southall about a month later and Ernie Kendall expresses no regrets at all that it ended when it did:

> When we got to the 'Jam 'Ole', the foreman said he had some bad news; he said it was the last trip. 'Bloody good job', I said. It was the best thing that ever happened when they told us we were redundant; it was hard going and it was never paid for, three on yer working for one's money. Thinking the hours as you'd done and the money you was a getting, you weren't getting many coppers an hour for it. Now you work till knockin' off time and that's fair enough; you travel home and you think to yourself, 'Well, that's the end of that day done'. When you're on trading boats, you're a doing seven days a week and you never used to count the hours. None of us never missed it, we just felt, 'Well good, save us keep going up and down'. Save us keep going up and down you see.

133

Some pockets of short haul traffic survived amidst the explosion of holiday cruising, and various attempts at a revival have been made but, after 200 years, long distance narrow boat carrying on England's canals was dead.

49 The last load to Croxley. Ted Ward operating the ancient crane with the disused unloading equipment behind

10

No Going Back

We began transferring the coal into *Barnham* and *Angel* at 7am and by 8.30, the sun was beating down mercilessly. We attacked the 22 tonnes from either end. John, accustomed to bagging up on his own, worked alone in *Comet*'s bow while Ian, Graham, my wife Heather and I (Pat and I were divorced in 1977), formed a team in the stern. At any one time, three of the four bagged up; the first man shovelled the coal into a half hundredweight bag held by the second man, who lifted it onto the scales when it was full. The third man weighed it, adding or taking out a few pieces where necessary, and stacked it. These tasks were rotated every twenty bags so that we utilised different muscles and eased the strain. The fourth man in the team lifted the bags overside with Sue, who got through a prodigious amount of work despite having to attend to Josh, and Marion, who was pregnant, kept us alive with an endless flow of liquid refreshment.

At mid-day, slumping onto the pile of empty sacks on the towpath, we appeared to have made little impression on the mountain in *Comet*'s hold and John's prediction that it might take a week to empty the boats, considered at the time to be a gross over estimation by the rest of us, was beginning to look horribly accurate. It was exhausting work in the scorching sun, the back ached and the fingers were sore behind the nails from gripping and lifting the full plastic sacks, but we reluctantly got to our feet and set to again, helped on our way by a drunk and jocular Irishman who ceremoniously presented us with a large bottle of cider in recognition of our industry.

By evening, *Angel* was stacked to the gunnels and *Comet* was empty. We washed off the worst of the grime under a tap by the locks and shambled off to bed, only too aware that the whole, painful process would have to be repeated with *Barnes'* load the very next day.

We had lost Heather to her job, which meant that we would have to interrupt the bagging to haul the sacks overside, but the day was overcast and cool and we were well practiced now in the art. Working from both ends as before, we toiled through the morning rain, but retreated to a caff in the High Street at lunch-time depressed once more by the quantity of coal still dividing us. But the honest fare seemed to revive our spirits and we strode purposefully back to the boats, determined to see the job done before the day was out. We set about the coal with a vengeance and by tea time, it was done. We had filled, weighed and transhipped around 1,650 half hundredweight bags. All that remained was to hose out the holds and mop down the paint work, and to reflect on the journey and what I had found in my search for the cut.

We had proved, first and foremost, that it could be done; that it was still possible to carry a decent sized load on the route that had seen the last regular narrow boat trade and that it could be achieved in a time considered acceptable in the sixties.

After going aground at Hillmorton, we realised that we would have to adapt to the changed contours of the cut for, with no working boats gouging a road and pleasure craft constantly cutting off corners, the canals tended to be uniformly shallow. Apart from Hillmorton, the Oxford was better than anticipated, but the Grand Union, particularly the southern end, had many more treacherous places than I remember. There was a lot of silting where streams entered the cut, as at Leighton Buzzard, and we were fortunate to have somebody off the boats when we got stuck in the middle; I think that Pat and I, with no extra hand, would still have been floundering below Grove Lock. But if another pair had followed us down a couple of days later, they would have benefited from our passage and would not have got stuck in half the places we did.

Paddle gear was generally workable, although many of the gate paddles had been removed, presumably for economic reasons, and this made locking a lot slower. Our main concern, however, was pleasure boats! When I was boating in the sixties, such craft were in a minority on a system still geared for trade and they got out of the way pretty smartly when they encountered working boats; now, the position is reversed. In total isolation, we had the uneasy feeling of imposing on a 'cruiseway'.

The significance of a loaded pair was completely lost on many hirers and owners. Some were visibly thrilled by the spectacle but, understandably, they were unaware of the factors governing the passage of working boats; the fact that we were obliged, for example, because of our deeper draught, to occupy the centre of the canal, where we hoped to find a little more water, was not appreciated.

Hirers who had left their boatyards on the same afternoon tended to travel in groups of two or three feeling, no doubt, that there was safety in numbers; but it didn't help at all when, seeing our approach, the leading skipper slowed to a stop and engaged neutral, thereby losing what little control he had over his craft. The second boat, inevitably, ran into the first and ricochetted into the path of our oncoming motor. I can just hear the hirers' protests on returning to their respective bases: 'It was them coal boats, they were to blame'. In the end, we treated the collisions as something of a game, awarding points for each impact or near miss, but the total number of bumps we received was, probably, only comparable to those totted up by any first time hirer going through his first lock.

We always slowed down approaching moored craft, but the volume of water displaced by the loaded boats caused one or two inadequately bedded mooring stakes to be uprooted when we passed. On one occasion, a very irate owner leaped out of his smart new tug style craft waving his fist and shouting abuse as *Comet* set his fore end adrift. When *Barnes* passed a few seconds later, his wife smiled sweetly and declared, 'That's much more civilised, at least *you're* going slowly'!

There were obvious and startling physical changes along the cut. The sprawl of Milton Keynes where, previously, there had been open fields; a void where Dickinson's massive Croxley Mill had stood; and evidence, at places like Stoke Bruerne, that over

50   Our main concern – pleasure boats!

commercialisation is destroying many of the aesthetic qualities that attracted people to the canals in the first place. With the coming of the leisure industry, the character of the cut has undergone a profound and undeniable transformation, but along the more inaccessible stretches, and even at the popular spots during 'off peak' times, it was still possible to enjoy its quiet beauty. And once in a while, in the back bar of the 'Greyhound', or at the Willow Wren yard at Braunston, the old atmosphere of boating life touched the senses.

It was the presence of the old boaters, more even than the surviving buildings or the restored narrow boats, that reminded one most eloquently of the past. At the end, they were poorly paid and dispirited, and those I spoke to insisted that they were happy when carrying ended; but they stick close to the water unwilling, or unable, to leave the cut completely behind. The Brays live on *Poacher* at Braunston, the Wards near Hawkesbury, with Ted sliding off to the cut whenever his vehicle delivery job takes him within range; and the ex-Willow Wren boaters take their holidays on the canals. The cut has changed irrevocably and they have accepted the change graciously, even eagerly. I too have accepted that leisure is king, for the trip made it plain that there is no going back.

But it was, truly, an adventure and as time goes by, I think I may cherish it just as much as those days in the sixties, when trade was enjoying its last, desperate fling on the canals of England.

Notes and references

Prelude: Old Boats – Hotel Boats (pages 11 to 22)
1 Gongoozlers – a term used to describe those who stand idly watching boats on the canal.
2 Peter Froud – after a long illness, Peter Froud died in hospital on 10th November 1986.
3 Ray White – Ray died suddenly at Leicester on 29th April 1987

Chapter One: *Comet* (pages 23 to 34)
1 Admiral class narrow boats – the majority of Admiral class boats were built by Isaac Pimblott & Sons of Northwich, for British Waterways' North West fleet and were named after admirals from Anson to Mountbatten. Cabins were made of steel and the holds were covered by drawing canvas sheets over low steel hoops. Their vertically stemmed bows tended to plough through the water, so a later version was built with a raked stem.

Chapter Two: *Barnes* – **And a Cargo** (pages 35 to 40)
1 Joyce and Peter Fox – the Foxes retired to their seaside home at Lymington in Hampshire at the close of the 1985 season.

Chapter Three: Buckby Wharf (pages 41 to 44)
1 Rolt, L. T. C. *Narrow Boat* (1944)
2 Streat, Michael. 'Buckby Can Shop Closes', *Waterways World*, Vol 7 Issue 6 (1978).

Chapter Four: Willow Wren (pages 45 to 60)
1 Morton, Leslie. 'The Willow Wren Group', Inland Waterways Association *Bulletin*, July 1965
2 *Bulletin*, May 1963

Chapter Five: Loading at Hawkesbury (pages 61 to 76)

1 Ovaltine boats – Wander Ltd, the producers of 'Ovaltine', ran a fleet of narrow boats between 1925 and 1959, which carried coal from the Warwickshire coalfield to the company's factory beside the Grand Union at Kings Langley. The boats were floating advertisements for the product and were immaculately painted in dark blue, edged with maroon and white, with orange and yellow lettering.
2 Coventry City Council and Nuneaton Borough Council. *Hawkesbury Junction Conservation Area.*

Chapter Six: Boaters and Boating (pages 77 to 94)

1 cratch – triangular board and wooden framework covered with tarpaulin at the for end of the hold for storing ropes, etc.
2 cants – wooden ledges running back from the stem along the foredeck on a narrow boat's bow
3 Blagrove, David. *Bread Upon the Waters* (Burton-on-Trent 1984)
4 Brigadier Fred Fielding – Brigadier Fielding died in the Spring of 1987

Chapter Seven: Life Afloat pages 95 to 112)

1 British Waterways Board. *Blisworth Tunnel Re-opened*, a supplement to *Waterways News*, August 1984
2 Blagrove, David. *Bread Upon the Waters*
3 Inland Waterways Association National Rally, Milton Keynes, *Souvenir Brochure*, August 1985

Chapter Eight: Past All the Old Places . . . To Brentford (pages 113 to 127)

1 John Barnes – in June 1984, after a 2–0 defeat by Russia at Wembley, when manager Bobby Robson was criticised for playing two wingers (considered a luxury in the modern game), the England team embarked on a tour of South America. A week later, in the massive Maracana Stadium, they beat the 'unbeatable' Brazilians and John Barnes, one of Robson's

vilified wingers, scored a stunning solo goal. From just inside
the Brazilian half, Barnes set off on a bewildering run through
the opposing defence, finally scoring from six yards; and
England went on to record their first win over the South
Americans on Brazilian soil.

APPENDIX I

Origins of the Narrow Boat

To understand the origins of the canal narrow boat, it is necessary to go back to the mid-eighteenth century, when roads in England were poor and the carriage of goods by pack-horse or cart was slow and expensive.

In 1759, in order to overcome the problem, the enterprising Duke of Bridgewater engaged mill-wright James Brindley to build a canal from his mines at Worsley, to Manchester. Subsequently extended to Runcorn, the canal was level (apart from a flight of ten locks down to the tidal Mersey), with an adequate supply of water and was built to accommodate the existing local craft known as Mersey flats, which measured approximately 70ft × 14ft beam.

While he was still working on the Bridgewater Canal, Brindley was approached by Josiah Wedgwood to build a waterway to link the rivers Trent and Mersey, an ambitious project which raised new engineering problems. Using a series of locks, the canal had to cross a high water-shed between the river valleys and penetrate, by means of a tunnel, Harecastle Hill at the summit.

It is probable that two factors, finance and the need to conserve water, dictated the dimensions of the waterway. In order to keep costs at a reasonable level, Brindley decided that the 2,880 yard tunnel should be only 8ft 6in wide, and as each boat crossing the summit level would use two locks of water (one ascending and one descending), which would have to be replenished, he built the locks half the width of those on the Bridgewater. The tunnel bore and the size of the lock chambers governed the dimensions of the craft able to navigate the canal, and so the narrow boat was born.

The 70ft × 7ft wooden boats were built with a square-sectioned hull to accommodate the maximum amount of cargo, combined with a graceful bow and stern which enabled the craft to swim well when towed by a horse, and to steer efficiently.

The boatman employed another man, or a boy, to drive the horse, and as the canal network grew and journeys became longer, it was necessary for a small cabin to be built at the stern end of the boat as living accommodation. During periods of slump on the canals, this 8ft × 7ft cabin became home for the boatman's wife and family, who were co-opted as crew to save the wages of a mate.

Steam and, later, internal combustion engines were installed and iron and steel largely replaced wood as construction materials. The motorised boats were able to tow an unpowered craft, making it possible to carry almost twice as much cargo with a two-person crew. Many boat people managed to keep a house 'on the land', but between the two World Wars, it became necessary for many families to live permanently on the boats.

The boats that impressed me so much during that first trip in 1957, were probably part of British Waterways' North West Division Southern carrying fleet, taking flour and sugar between Ellesmere Port and Birmingham, and lubricating oil from Stanlow to Wolverhampton.

APPENDIX II

Brief descriptions of narrow boat types

Fellows, Morton & Clayton Ltd was one of the largest and best known carrying companies prior to nationalisation in 1948. Their boats were known as 'Joshers', after company director Joshua Fellows, and were built at the company's own yard at Saltley, Birmingham, or by Yarwoods of Northwich. 'Joshers' have the most elegant bow shape; little freeboard when fully loaded; high cratch, mast and stands; and rectangular, panelled cabin sides. *Hawk* was built at Yarwoods in 1927 of iron composite construction (ie iron sides, elm bottom) and was fitted out at Uxbridge.

The Shropshire Union Railway & Canal Co developed a substantial fleet of narrow boats, many operating fast services for the conveyance of agricultural produce. These craft have fine lines with long, sleek fore-decks, and a carrying capacity of only 18 tons. *Saturn* was built of English oak and elm in 1906, and carried cheeses to Manchester from the canal-side farms of Shropshire and Cheshire.

Small Woolwich boats were built at Harland & Wolfe's yard at Woolwich during the 1930s, for the Grand Union Canal Carrying Co. They are of composite construction (iron or steel sides, elm bottom) and are known as Star Class, being named after stars and planets.

Station boats were built by Yarwoods for the London Midland & Scottish Railway for use as day boats between canal-side factories and canal-railway interchange basins. Originally horse-drawn, they are of wooden or composite construction and have fine lines with long, flattish bow decks. Because of their very low freeboard, cabins, when fitted, looked exceptionally high. *Dabchick* was one of the last 'station boats' trading.

Large Woolwich boats built for the Grand Union fleet are of all steel construction and are known as Town Class, being named after British towns and villages. These boats have very deep holds and when they are empty, with their bluff bows out of the water, they are an imposing looking craft.

APPENDIX III

A brief account of the rebuilding of *Comet* by Ian Kemp

Replacement of fore-end cants and deck ledge.

Replacement of fore-end bulkhead. Replacement of beams, saddles and all gunwhales, running planks, cratch, false cratch and uprights.

Replacement of engine room roof and bottom half of engine room/cabin bulkhead. Replacement of counter, helm tube, counter top and counter bottom.

Complete replacement of cabin, cabin floor, and all internal cabin fitments.

The cabin was completely rewired and the wiring to the head-lamp was replaced.

Removal of Lister HA2 and replacement with Petter PD2. Renewal of tailshaft, intermediate shaft, and all shaft bearings. Change of propeller.

All controls renewed – push/pull gear change replaced by wheel gear change.

Complete repaint to the livery typical of a standard British Waterways carrying craft of the late 1950s.

I have fitted approximately 40ft of new elm bottom, and have had the corroded areas of platework shot blasted.

A new set of side cloths have been fitted to the boat and a new set of tipcats.

APPENDIX IV

Roger Alsop's payment slips and a consignment note for Willow Wren trips

Opposite and on the following pages are reproduced payment slips of the kind received by Roger Alsop at the end of each of his working trips, showing not only deductions for tax and insurance but also for any items of gear for the boat, and of course its hire from the owners. Each slip also had a corresponding consignment note, an example of which is reproduced on page 154.

R. ALLSOPP   29.7.64

COAL Newdigate/C. Valley   49 11 × 14/= = £34.13.8

Helping Jo Empty   10 - 0

                                                £35 · 3 · 8

Less

Hire of braft. 1 (LOAD)   £1·0·0
Towards Reserve bredit   £5·0·0
N.1. 2 wks. "/8 to 27/7/64   1 - 3 4
mate   " 9/8 — " —   19·4
Income TAX.   1· 4· 0
mate   1· 4· 0
Towards Refund baler booker   1·3·0   £ 11 - 13 - 8
(BAL. £4·17·0)   £23 ·10· 0

Reserve bredit £5

R. ALSOP   16-11-64

T. cwts
COAL. Newdigate / Ricky   50-2 × 14/= per ton   £35 - 1 . 5 .
Discharging   "   × 3/=   7 . 10 . 3 .
Empty   10 . 0 .
                                               ————————
                                               £43 . 1 . 8

Less

HIRE OF CRAFT (LOAD)   £1 - 0 0 .

ADVANCE HAWKESBURY   7 . 0 . 0 .

4/9/64 1· Chimney   1 - 12 . 6 .

Starting money last Sett.   5

Towards Reserve Credit   5 . 0 . 0

3 wks N. I × 11/8 To 16/1   1 - 15 . 0

mate   " × 9/8 — w.   1 - 9 . 0

TAX.   17 . 0 .   18 - 13 - 11
                                             ————————
                                             24 - 7 - 9

            STARTING MONEY   2 . 3
                                             ————————
                                             £24 - 10 - 0
                                             ════════

(Reserve Credit £40)

13

R. ALSOP.   28·10·64.

TOMATO PUREE B'F). B'HAM. T.cwts 49·8 × 13/= per ton £32·2·2

Less

Hire of broght. I LOAD).	£1·0·0
ADVANCE BULLS BRIDGE	2·0·0
16/10/64 TKT 2. 20 galls fuel × 1/7	1·11·8 .
STARTING money lost Sett.	1·11 .
Towards Reserve bredit	5·0·0 .
3 wks N 1 × 11/8 To 26/10/64	1·15·0
mofe -"- × 9/8 —"—	1·9·0 .
TAX .	5·0 Refund =. 12·12·7

£ 19·9·7

STARTING money.   5

£ 19·10·0

(Reserve bredit £35)

17

R. ALSOP.   28.1.65

Timber B/(F) – Nottingham. 24 Tons x 25/=   £30. 0. 0.
Loading   ———   ——. 4/= .   4. 16. 0.

PLUS. Working for BBC. 2 days   10. 0. 0
                                           £44 - 16 - 0

Less

Hire of braft (Load)   £1 - 0 0 .
16/1/65 Advance B/Bdge.   5. 0 0.
22/1/65   "   "   7. 0 0.

Starting money last Sett.   5 - 10 .
to Ad.9.
Injection Pipe. Filter + Element. 1 - 13. 6.⎫
Labour.   1 - 13. 6.⎬
MILEAGE.   12 0 ⎭.

N.I. 4 wks x 11/8 to 25/1/65. 2. 6. 8.
mate   "   x 9/8 ——.   1 - 18. 8.
30/12/64 TKT 52 1 gall Lub x 8/=   8. 0
22/1/65 TKT 47 25 glls fuel x 1/7 . 1 - 19 . 7
         1 gll. Lub x 8/= per gll   8 0 .

Refund of 2 glls Lub ex TKT 52. 2/12/64 16. 0 Refund .
TAX .   1. 9. 0 Refund .

Towards Special Reserve   5 - 0 0 .   £27. 0. 9
Reserve credit £50 ⎫
+ Special   £5 ⎬   STARTING MONEY   £ 17 - 15. 3
                                              4   9
                                          £18 - 0 - 0

WILLOW WREN CANAL TRANSPORT SERVICES LTD.

BULLS BRIDGE
HAYES ROAD
SOUTHALL, MIDDLESEX

Telephone: HAYes 2277-8

Messrs. _West Herts Drainage Board_

23rd July 1904.

RICKMANSWORTH

Ref. No.

Please receive the undermentioned goods from Messrs. _Rickdgete Jackling_
per our craft _"ECHET" + DARENTH" -_ _Steerer R Allen_

QUANTITY	DESCRIPTION	WEIGHT		
		T	C	Q
	Coal	49	11	1

Received the above in good condition

All Goods carried subject to the Company's Conditions of Carriage

155

APPENDIX V

Log of 1985 trip

Date	Departure	Arrival	Duration	Distance*	No of locks
Fri 19 July	Hawkesbury 17.45	Newbold 23.30	5hrs 45min	11m 4f	1
Sat 20	Newbold 07.30	Stoke Bruerne 22.15	14hrs 45min	31m 1½f	16
Sun 21	Stoke Bruerne 06.30	Leighton Buzzard 19.30	13hrs	26m 2f	14
Mon 22	Leighton Buzzard 10.30	Bourne End 22.30	12hrs	17m 0½f	32
Tue 23	Bourne End 06.00	Southall 20.00	14hrs	25m 1¾f	30
Wed 24	Southall 09.30	Brentford 12.30	3hrs	4m 3f	10
			62hrs 30min	115m 4¾f	103

* Distance in miles and furlongs.

APPENDIX VI

Full list of trips completed by Roger Alsop for Willow Wren

	Cargo	Loading at	Destination	Consigment note date
1	Coal	Newdigate Colliery	West Herts Drainage Board Rickmansworth	23.7.64
2	Aluminium ingots	Brentford	Tyseley Wharf, Birmingham	6.8.64
3	Coal	Baddesley Colliery	Rickmansworth	20.8.64
4	Timber	Brentford	West Bromwich	28.8.64
5	Coal	North Warwick Colliery	Croxley Mills	16.9.64
6	Coal	North Warwick	Croxley Mills	7.10.64
7	Tomato puree	Brentford	Sampson Road, Birmingham	21.10.64
8	Coal	Newdigate	Rickmansworth	13.11.64
9	Timber	Brentford	West Bromwich	1.12.64
10	Coal	North Warwick	Croxley Mills	18.12.64
11	Timber	Brentford	Nottingham	28.1.65 (pay slip date)
12	Coal	North Warwick	Croxley Mills	11.2.65 (pay slip date)

Trips 1 to 7 – *Comet* and *Dabchick*.
Trips 8 to 12 *Comet* and *Barnes*.

156

APPENDIX VII

Ted Ward's payment slip for the last run undertaken by Willow Wren boats

2/10/70   *T. WARD*   99

Coal Gopsall to Croxley			
45tons 9cwt @ 11/9	£26	14s	6d
Light running	2	10	0
	29	4	6
Craft hire 27/7/70 to 4/10/70			
40 days @ 3/-	6	0	0
Advance	10	0	0
NI 3/10/17/24/31 8/10			
5 @ 17/8	4	8	4
60 galls diesel	5	0	0
	25	8	4
	£3	16	2

Bibliography

Barnes, Richard. *Mods* (Eel Pie Publishing 1979)

Blagrove, David. *Bread Upon the Waters* (J. M. Pearson & Son 1984)

British Waterways Board. *The Future of the Waterways* (1964) *Blisworth Tunnel Re-opened* (Supplement to *Waterways News*, August 1984)

Chaplin, Tom. *A Short History of the Narrow Boat* (Hugh McKnight Publications 1967) *The Narrow Boat Book* (Whittet Books 1978)

Chapman, F. J. J. *'The Boatman's Institute'* (Waterways World, Vol 2 No 12)

Coventry Canal Society. *Coventry's Waterways – A City Amenity* (1972)

Faulkner, Alan. *'The Willow Wren Story'* (Waterways World, Vol 12 Nos 8 & 9) *The George and the Mary* (Robert Wilson Publications 1973)

Hadfield, Charles. *British Canals* (David & Charles 1979)

Inland Waterways Association. *Bulletin.* Specifically issues of the period covered by this book.

Melly, George. *Revolt Into Style – The Pop Arts In Britain* (Penguin 1970)

Ministry of Transport. *British Waterways: Recreation and Amenity* (White Paper) (HMSO 1967)

Rolt, L. T. C. *Narrow Boat* (Methuen 1944)

Streat, Michael. *'Buckby Can Shop Closes'* (Waterways World, Vol 7 No 6) *'The Waterways World of Braunston'* (Waterways World Vol 7 No 9)

Ware, M. E. *Narrow Boats at Work* (Moorland Publishing 1980)

Webb, Mike. *Braunston's Boats* (J. M. Pearson & Son 1983)

Wheen, Francis. *The Sixties* (Century Publishing 1982)

Wilson, Robert J. *Epilogue* (Robert Wilson Publications 1977) *Life Afloat* (Robert Wilson Publication 1976) *Too Many Boats* (Robert Wilson Publications 1980)

Acknowledgements

Special thanks are due to Cathy, whose indulgence was endless when it was far from easy. We are grateful to Heather, Ian and Marion, and Sue and John for their commitment to the idea and its execution; David Vickers for trusting us with his boat; and Harry Arnold for the professionalism which produced dozens of memorable pictures – the majority of which could not be used due to lack of space. With sincere apologies to anyone we may have overlooked, we would also like to thank the following for their contributions: Andy Davey, David Harris, Sue and Keith Tagg, Tony and Trevor Jones, Dennis Clarke, Ted Ward, Chris Barney, Shirley Ginger, Mike Webb, Ernie Kendall, Joyce and Peter Fox, Peter Froud, Ruth and David Lucy, David Humphries, Clive Stevens, David Blagrove, The Fosters, and the staff at the IWA, Regent's Park and the Waterways Museum, Stoke Bruerne.